PRAISE FOR
The FINAL SUMMIT

Every generation or so, God produces a person who can communicate like no one else. His words are like cool water to a thirsty civilization. Andy Andrews is one of the best I have ever seen.

—Zig Ziglar,
America's #1 motivator and best-selling author

Is it possible to mix C. S. Lewis, Alfred Hitchcock, and Tony Robbins? *The Final Summit* is a unique and powerful blend of mystery and suspense and principles and emotional fire. Wow! Bring your highlighter to this party. You'll want to remember every word!

—Hal Sutton,
PGA champion

This is no ordinary author. Andy Andrews is a Life Whisperer. He has a way of taking life's most confusing issues and simplifying them, allowing us to harness principles and reach our fullest potential. *The Final Summit* is his best work yet . . . and that's really saying something!

—Dave Ramsey,
Nationally syndicated radio host and
best-selling author of *The Total Money Makeover*

Have you given up in some area of your life? If it were possible, would you change something about "the way you are"? If so, *The Final Summit* is for you. Read this book now.

—Patsy Clairmont,
Speaker and author of *Kaleidoscope*

People who don't like to read LOVE Andy Andrews' books. Think about that for a minute. Surely, there is no higher praise.

—Sandi Patty,
Grammy Award–winning recording artist

This is not another "celebrity author" or "motivational guy." People love Andy Andrews because his words change their lives. And those words have been carefully excavated from his own heart.

—Joe Bonsall,
The Oak Ridge Boys

Once again, Andy Andrews draws us into the narrative with his masterful storytelling. But this is not ordinary fiction. Drawing from history, science, and religion, The Final Summit frames our individual challenge to make a difference. If you're comfortable with complacency or blaming, you'll be uncomfortable reading this book.

—Dan Miller,
author 48 Days to the Work You Love

The journey through The Final Summit and The Traveler's Gift has allowed me to take on more than I ever thought I was capable of doing.

—Lenny Sisselman,
LSA Entertainment

Under a master storyteller's hand, history comes alive, and speaks to us all.

—Howie Klausner,
Writer, Space Cowboys

The Final Summit is a crucial piece of literature for our times. Andy Andrews once again weaves an important, entertaining, and profound story imbued with a fundamental message that both challenges and inspires. If you liked The Traveler's Gift, you will love and appreciate this book!

—Scott Carr,
Director of Development, Hollywood Gang Production

A captivating climb to a crucial choice led by a collection of the most inspirational minds of all time, and one spellbinding story teller.

—John Wilder,
Award-winning writer/producer

This is the book that the entire world has been waiting on someone to write. Thank you, Andy Andrews.

—Jonathan Burleson,
Director of National Sales, Gaylord Hotels

Andy possesses the rare ability to entertain and enlighten at the same time. *The Final Summit* is evidence enough. Through laughter, sighs, chill bumps, and tears, you'll lose track of time, learn about the world, and reflect on your life. Give it to yourself. Then give it to a friend.

—Gary Keller,
New York Times best-selling author of
SHIFT: How Top Agents Tackle Tough Times;
Cofounder and Chairman of the Board,
Keller Williams Realty

Once again, Andy Andrews delivers chills, laughter, and tears. *The Final Summit* is a masterpiece for our generation.

—Don Reid, The Statler Brothers

For six years now, Andy Andrews' words have influenced and greatly impacted every single Air Force Special Operations squadron at every location they occupy around the world. He is our "go-to" guy as we raise up new generations of leaders!

—Lt. General (Ret.) Mike Wooley,
Air Force Special Operations Commander

OTHER BOOKS BY ANDY ANDREWS

The FINAL

SUMMIT

A QUEST TO FIND THE ONE PRINCIPLE

THAT WILL SAVE HUMANITY

ANDY ANDREWS

THOMAS NELSON
Since 1798

NASHVILLE DALLAS MEXICO CITY RIO DE JANEIRO

Published in Nashville, Tennessee, by Thomas Nelson. Thomas Nelson is a registered trademark of Thomas Nelson, Inc.

Thomas Nelson, Inc., titles may be purchased in bulk for educational, business, fund-raising, or sales promotional use. For information, please e-mail SpecialMarkets@ThomasNelson.com.

The Scripture quotation on the epigraph page is paraphrased in the author's words.

Chapter 1 mentions *Soul of the Lion: A Biography of General Joshua L. Chamberlain* by Willard M. Wallace (Gettysburg, PA: Stan Clark Military Books, 1996).

Chapter 4 mentions *The Principle of the Path: How to Get from Where You Are to Where You Want to Be* by Andy Stanley (Nashville: Thomas Nelson, 2009).

ISBN 978-0-8499-4866-4 (ie)

Library of Congress Cataloging-in-Publication Data

Andrews, Andy, 1959-
   The final summit : a quest to find the one principle that will save humanity / Andy Andrews.
     p. cm.
   ISBN 978-0-7852-3120-2 (hardcover)
 1. Conduct of life. 2. Principle (Philosophy) I. Title.
BJ1597.A518 2010
813'.6—dc22

2010034235

Printed in the United States of America

11 12 13 14 QGF 9 8 7 6 5 4 3 2 1

To Kathy and Dick Rollins
of Columbus, Mississippi.
I will always be grateful for your
influence and example.

For I am but a Traveler upon this earth.

—DAVID (PSALM 39:12)

PROLOGUE

It is amazing, isn't it, how one sound can distinguish itself from another? When the hustle-and-bustle around us is intrusive and overwhelming, how do our minds separate from the din that solitary ring tone? Or how, on a playground vibrating with the chatter of youngsters, do we manage to quickly distinguish the single voice of our own child?

It was with those curious thoughts easing in and out of his mind that Carl Santiago looked up from the security desk. After all, it was almost time to close, which meant that dozens of workers were flooding the lobby, ready to leave for the day. Among them, Carl knew, was Gloria, who would be departing at the end of her shift. Still, he marveled at his ability to pick out the distinct sound of her high heels clicking across the marble floor of the lobby.

Carl's desk—it was actually a huge block of granite—was situated near the entrance and had been carved and placed in such a manner as to "flow" into the koi pond. At least that is how he remembered the architect describing it. Carl had been the first security officer, hired before the structure was even erected. He was part of the security for the foreman's staff during the construction years, and when the work was completed,

1

he walked right into the boss's office and declared himself a part of the place and "in for life."

It had been amazing to watch the building climb the Dallas skyline while the media heckled and scoffed at its owner. *The old guy* was *a bit eccentric,* Carl admitted to himself. The man did things and said things and lived in a manner that was not entirely ordinary—that was for sure. But Carl *liked* the owner of the building. Yes, the man was in his seventies now, but his life had produced what Carl called "fruit on the tree."

Carl had been in his late twenties when it all started. He and his wife had just welcomed a newborn baby into a world that seemed to terrify them. Neither Carl nor his wife had been traditionally educated. They emigrated legally from Mexico after months of waiting and paperwork, struggling with the language a bit but working hard, saving everything beyond what was needed for necessities.

Carl met the owner of the building during its first construction phase. The owner was a wealthy man who had been rich before. Carl had read all about him in the newspapers. The man had made a fortune by the age of fifty-five but lost every dime of it in a very public way when his debts overcame him.

According to the press, this man had "a magic touch." The media seemed to make a connection between the man's temperament and his money. True enough, when Carl met him, his personality *was* buoyant. He was down-to-earth and extremely likable. At the time of their first meeting, the man was sixty-something and had already come back from his financial difficulties. Way back. And everyone knew it. After all, it had been on the national news. This guy—a man who had gone bankrupt—had made *another* fortune and repaid every single creditor! And he had not been forced to do it.

The man was fabulously wealthy, but one might never have known. In fact, when Carl met him, the man had been wearing blue jeans and a burnt-orange Texas Longhorns sweatshirt. He had driven onto the property after hours in a Ford F-350 Diesel, and Carl stopped him—just as he had been trained to do. Carl *was* security for the job site, after all.

"Good evening, sir," Carl had said. "How can I help you?"

The man opened the truck door, put a beautifully made (but atrociously dirty) M. L. Leddy boot on the ground, and answered, "Sir yourself! If you have a moment, I would like *you* to show me around."

Carl quickly recognized the man from television and the newspapers. He was the owner of the whole place. Nevertheless, Carl politely asked the man for identification, and politely the man produced it, smiling and adding a "Thanks" for that slightly uncomfortable job well done.

It had been that day when the man made a casual remark to Carl that was soon to cause a firestorm of controversy. "I'm not going to borrow a dollar to build this place," the man had said as he kicked a rock with his boot. "Not one dang dollar."

"Okay," Carl said in return. He hadn't known how he was supposed to respond. Carl had never met a rich guy before.

3

"How old are you?" the man asked Carl. When Carl told him, the man went into a long speech about "paying as you go" and "not getting your cart before your horse." The man reminded Carl of his grandfather back in Mexico. Carl had smiled and nodded then, not knowing how else to act.

When finally they came back to the man's truck, he shook hands with Carl and told him, "I'm not kidding. Don't borrow any money." He laughed and nodded, and the wealthy man drove away.

But Carl never did borrow any money. At first, it was easy. No one would have loaned him anything anyway. Carl considered himself blessed—lucky, his cousins said—to have become friends with the wealthy man. Carl learned some principles from the man; he paid as he went, and his family now lived in a nice home that was totally paid off. And just last week, Carl and his wife had celebrated another anniversary with what seemed to Carl like *a lot* of money in the bank.

Through the years, the wealthy man had never forgotten Carl's name. Nor had he ever neglected to spark a conversation when the opportunity presented itself. Once, the man had even broken through a mass of people that included a media line to introduce the president of the United States . . . to him. To Carl.

Carl and his wife had laughed when they watched the news that night. "Mr. President," the man had said, "I'd like you to meet my good friend Carl." Good friend. How about that? The owner of the building where he worked had called him a "good friend" in front of the entire world!

But that was then and this was now. Carl shook his head to clear the memories. The security for the building had been increased some years ago after 9/11. Thus, the desk itself was now joined with water to provide what amounted to a beautiful barrier to the six glass elevators that were perched amid palms and waterfalls flowing around the desk and into the pond. This incredible obstruction enabled Carl and the other security staff to funnel, register, photograph, badge, and track every single person who entered the fifty-five-story office building.

To say that the lobby was large would be an understatement. The building's first five floors were an atrium that covered a city block. Forty-foot palms and live oak trees stood near each other, highlighted by a stream running from one corner of the edifice to the other. Grassy areas and flower beds were adorned with comfortable tables and chairs. In fact, many of the building's occupants took lunch there. It looked more like a park than a place of business.

All the beauty and grandeur of the entrance, while visible from the elevators or even outside the building, were *behind* security. In fact, the only office *not* behind barriers was the one that oversaw the establishment's massive parking deck. And it was that very office from which the sound of three-inch spiked heels began to emanate as Gloria Jackson made her way across the lobby floor.

Carl looked up and smiled. "Ms. Jackson," he said to greet her.

"Mr. Santiago," she replied brightly. Some unseen button was evidently pushed as a section of the granite desk folded smoothly into the floor, allowing the attractive woman to walk smartly across it. As soon as she had done so, the granite piece returned to its previous level, sliding into place with a satisfying *thunk*. Gloria Jackson was now behind the security desk.

Tall and beautifully proportioned, her skin was the color of caramel and rippled as she walked, the muscle tone apparent in her legs and arms. Gloria was almost sixty years old but could—and often did—pass for a woman in her forties. She ran transportation for the company in whatever incarnation that might mean at any particular moment. Helicopter to DFW, private jet out of Grapevine, or a taxi to Bass Pro Shops—whether it was a sedan with a little extra room or a bulletproof, steel-reinforced hard car for the governor of Texas, Gloria was on it.

Her boss was the owner of the building. He was a man recognized in public, but very few people knew him like she did. Gloria and her husband, Martin, *understood* the man who existed beyond the impressions that had been formed by the media in recent years. He had hired them to work at his house years before, when his wife was alive. The man obviously invented work for Gloria and her husband back then, doing anything he could do to put money in the hands of the young parents. He knew they were penniless, but with his words and work, the man encouraged them.

When the man and his family lost their home, Gloria and

her husband continued to help—even when he had nothing to pay her. All the other staff left, of course. The man had told Gloria he was bankrupt. And he told her it was his own fault. That was all right, she figured. "I been broke too," she had smiled and told him.

But that was then. Now Gloria's husband worked in her department—transportation—and at that very moment, he was outside in the car, waiting for her to leave.

"Has the boss come down at all today?" Gloria asked Carl, who shook his head in reply. Her eyes drifted toward the elevator shaft. "This makes four days, Carl. He has been up there for four days. Is he okay?"

"Well . . . there's Internet traffic on his computer, and the sensors detect motion every now and then, so yeah, I guess he's okay *physically*, if that's what you mean." They shared a glance. "But he hasn't been up and down like usual."

"Well, he's got everything he needs," Gloria said, as if to remind herself. "Should we call Jenny? No, don't," Gloria asked and answered her own question. "I'm going home. Everyone knows how to get me if they need me. Are you staying, Carl?"

"I will, I think," Carl responded. He gestured over his shoulder at the other guards. "Their shift is starting. My guys have already gone, but I just feel . . . I don't know . . ."

Carl took Gloria by the arm and moved out of earshot of anyone else. Talking softly, he said, "Look, I would hate for something to be needed up there and then the folks responding not to be 'friends,' you know?" Carl glanced around nervously. "Is he all right, Gloria? Mentally, I mean? Is he okay? You know I love him. I hate to ask that, but . . ."

"Shh . . . Carl . . . it's okay. I know, I know." Gloria smiled sadly. "Just stay here if you can. And call if you need me. Good night," she said with a weak wave.

"Good night," Carl replied with a sigh as his eyes turned upward.

CHAPTER 1

Absently, the man rested his forearm on a piece of steel railing that, when he allowed himself to think about it, was the only thing separating him from life and—well, what came next. *Curious that I would think about it that way*, he thought. *I know what comes next.* With his thumb and forefinger, he played with a coffee bean he'd picked up in the kitchen. Cracking it with his thumbnail, he brought it to his nose.

His wife had loved the smell of coffee. With his eyes closed, he inhaled slowly. The pleasant aroma drifted through his imagination as it gained traction and took him to Peter Island in the Caribbean. He remembered their honeymoon, the sand on the beach, and the heavy fragrance of the Blue Mountain coffee that permeated every room in the resort.

They had gone back to the British Virgin Islands many times through the years. And they always stayed at the same place—Peter Island Resort. Even when they could have *bought* the resort, Ellen insisted they stay in one of the less expensive rooms, one like they had enjoyed so many years ago.

Years ago. How many years ago? David Ponder flicked the pieces of the coffee bean out into the night sky and turned to go back inside. Fifty-five stories. He was more than seven hundred feet up in the rarefied air of a warm Dallas night. Moving toward his front door, David started to go inside, but he stopped instead and sat down in a rocking chair on the porch.

"Seventy-four," David said aloud. "I am seventy-four years old. How . . . ?" David drew his hands up as if to use them for emphasis. But there was nothing to emphasize and no one to talk to, in any case, so he folded his hands back in his lap and closed his eyes.

David had been moderately successful as a young man, struggling early in his career with a new wife and a child. At one point, as an executive in his midforties, just when things seemed to be going well, he was laid off. The firing had been done in a cruel manner, and things seemed to go from bad to worse. But then, there had been an odd, singular event in David's life that had changed everything. It was what close friends and family referred to as "the accident." But it had been no accident—it had been a gift. And with his knowledge of the Seven Decisions for Success, David's fortunes had soared.

He knew that his time travel had been real. It was not a dream or hallucination as a result of coma from the automobile accident. The Seven Decisions he had gathered from the lives of the other Travelers had changed everything. Not just for David and Ellen, but for hundreds of thousands of others with whom he had gone on to share the decisions.

Working in real estate and as a developer, David had become hugely successful. In addition to the money he generously shared, he freely taught the principles he had used to create wealth. David became recognizable and was often referred to as an example of a rags-to-riches story. No doubt, he was on a roll. But David made a mistake. Call it what you will—a stock market debacle, a mortgage disaster, or a bad economy—David did the one thing his daddy had always told him *not* to do: he spent more money than he had. The lenders called the notes. And he was bankrupt at the age of fifty-five.

The boat, the cars, two houses, jewelry—Ellen's jewelry— had all disappeared. At first, he had been stunned. David stood in his yard one night and shouted at God. Oh, he knew God was there. *That* was no longer an issue. After all, he had been a Traveler. He—David Ponder—had accepted from the hands of history the very principles he had used to create a fortune. And now this?

David yelled. He screamed and cursed the air.

But God did not respond.

Their daughter, Jenny, had been home from college when the bankruptcy had been filed, and of course, she was terribly embarrassed. But there was nothing to be done. All their employees were gone—the lone exception being young Gloria Jackson and her husband, who took an apartment near the unit David and Ellen had secured for themselves. Jenny got a job in Austin, continued her education, and life went on.

David and Ellen worked here and there. He as a consultant or a facilitator, she as a neighborhood concierge—a "Girl Friday," she called herself. Financially, it was enough to get by.

Some nights David would bring out the tobacco pouch that he guarded carefully and rustle through its contents as if to convince himself one more time that, yes, it had all really happened.

Ellen didn't know *what* to think, really, during those dark days. She loved David, and while he had never told anyone else about his conversations with the people he referred to as "the Travelers"—he had told her. She wanted desperately to believe the crazy story he insisted on rehashing night after night. True, she did not have any idea where else in the world he might've found an antique tobacco pouch with seven priceless missives crammed into it. Or how he possibly could have gotten it all together that day. She had checked—there had been only twenty minutes between the time he'd been fired from Marshall's Hardware and the wreck.

Of course, craziest of all—the Seven Decisions had worked. That part of it was no secret. As David healed from the accident, he had become a different person, and eventually he began to make a lot of money. It all seemed to be a fairy tale come true . . . until their financial ruin.

But even the bankruptcy had its positive side. Ellen and David had reconnected in a way they had not experienced since college. They were closer—better friends than they had ever been—and "things" seemed not to matter as much as before. The media's barrage during the very public way their business failed had been tough, but it served to reveal a few true friends, and for that they were grateful.

"Adversity is preparation for greatness," David had said

suddenly to Ellen one night in their apartment. "Harry Truman told me that." Noting her surprised expression, he added, "You can sit there with your 'My husband is nuts' look if you want to, but I am going to take the man at his word!"

"Calm down, David," Ellen had replied evenly. "I don't think you're any crazier than I usually do, but what *are* you talking about?"

David explained excitedly. "One of the things President Truman told me when I . . ." He paused, still for an instant as he mentally edited. "Oh, you know what happened. Well, anyway . . ." David moved his hands quickly as if to erase his words, then continued, his thoughts bubbling up at once.

"Truman said . . ." David stopped again. "I didn't call him that, of course. I didn't call him 'Truman.' I called him Mr. President . . . Oh, whatever." David waved his hands again.

"'Adversity is preparation for greatness' is what the man said. He also talked to me about responsibility. And here is what I know about our current situation: I caused our adversity with a variety of bad choices. I have now learned from those bad choices. The Seven Decisions for Success that I used before are timeless. It was *my* lack of wisdom that caused the disaster, Ellen!

"So I am saying this. We are through with the 'adversity' part of this experience. Right now—tonight—I call an end to it. It is time to run again. We are not lacking money. We are not lacking time. We are not lacking energy or leadership. *We are only lacking an idea.*"

It had not been eloquent, but Ellen understood what her husband meant, and she was excited to see a fire in his eyes again. Within a few months, the idea David sought had come to him. It turned out to be a simple piece of software combining graph theory and aspect-oriented programming that allowed any business a way to integrate accounting strategies, billing procedures, and tax plans with any other business or client—from state to state or country to country.

"It was simple," David said to the *Dallas Morning News*. "I learned the concept in my tenth-grade algebra class. It's an idea anyone could have had. Honestly, I'm really not all that smart."

But smart or not, the idea had been worth a lot of money.

That one concept, combined with David's understanding and application of the Seven Decisions, paved the way to a creation of a whole new empire. Because this business wasn't tied to a particular "thing" like a house or a retail item, it was an entirely new way of adding value to the lives of people, whether they owned a large business or a small one. The software saved time, money, paper, and frustration—and because of it, Ponder International rose like a phoenix into the sky. How it happened was pure Texas legend.

After public negotiations and a zoning change that made the news, David bought property and announced plans for a fabulous skyscraper. Within five minutes of unveiling the artist's rendering for the city fathers, on camera, David declared to a disbelieving assemblage that the skyscraper would be built without a loan. "We will pay as we go" were his exact words. Immediately, without a vote, everyone decided that David Ponder was crazy. He had gone from hero to buffoon in one press conference.

At first, when they realized he was serious, no construction company would accept the contract. But he let the bidders wait until they were hungry, showed his money at the right time, and the white granite tower began to rise. Once, he stopped construction when cash reserves ran low—*that* made the news—but he had vowed never again to borrow any money. And he didn't.

When the tower was finished, the first thing David did was take the Ponder name off it. "This is not about me," he said when he cut the ribbon. "This is not about being the biggest or the first or the prettiest. This has been—and still is—about jobs for our area and working together as a community.

"I wanted to prove to myself—and some other folks in this country—that a big business can be run and major projects can be managed without debt or tragic disagreements between labor and management."

So David Ponder had won after all. Without a loan, he had erected a fifty-five-story building—one floor for each year of what he called his *first* financial life. Of course, at that point, the skyscraper was only a part of the Ponder fortune. Which made David's next financial move even more astounding. He gave it all away.

With expert legal help, David and Ellen Ponder created

foundations and charitable trusts around the world. Their daughter, Jenny, and her husband were tapped to oversee the whole thing.

David and Ellen retired. Except for occasional trips to the Caribbean and the speaking engagements David continued to do—most of them for free—the couple preferred to stay close to home. "Home" was the entire top floor of the skyscraper, a fabulous penthouse David had created for his wife. With Ellen's eye for interior design and a collection of furniture and art gathered during their years of travel, it was what they had always dreamed of: a place of beauty and privacy for their family and friends as they grew older.

The home, set above the city as it was, had become a source of curiosity for the media. Other than helicopter shots of the pool and a garden David had installed for Ellen, the penthouse itself had never been filmed or photographed.

David opened his eyes and sniffed loudly as he rocked, looking over the porch and pool. He gazed beyond the railing and saw the Magnolia Building with its trademark flying red horse on top. Over to the right glowed the green argon lights of the National Bank skyscraper. As a child, Jenny had called it the Jolly Green Giant. "Ho ho ho," David croaked, trying desperately not to sound as miserable as he felt.

Ellen had died eight months ago. Forty-nine years of being together and she'd gone without even saying good-bye. David opened his eyes wide, trying to keep the moisture in its place.

He frowned. Ellen hadn't even been sick. Didn't have so

much as a cold. Spent the night in Austin with Jenny and the grandkids and died in her sleep. Went to bed, didn't wake up. Well, David had tried to do the same thing for months now, but it wasn't working. He couldn't even die.

Feeling older than he usually felt, David shoved himself forward and got his feet under him. Standing up, he took one more look at the Jolly Green Giant and walked inside. He thought for a moment he might get a cup of coffee but decided against it and wandered into his office. Without thinking, he sat down in the chair behind his desk and reached for the safe door in the credenza. It wasn't locked. He never locked it. Didn't know why he'd let them put a safe there in the first place. He didn't even know the combination.

Having done it a thousand times, David reached to the back of the safe—*there . . . on the right side*—and retrieved a soft, blue tobacco pouch. Carefully, he placed it in his lap. Relaxing then, tension leaving his arms and legs, David leaned back in his chair; and with his fingers tenderly caress-ing the object that was so precious to him, he closed his eyes with purpose for the second time that night and allowed the memories, as they always did, to wash over him.

The tobacco pouch was navy blue and had been sewn from stout cloth, but the rough treatment it had received had worn the pouch to moleskin softness. It was beaten and threadbare but still handsome, regal in a sense, the possession of an offi-cer. The two buttons that closed the flap were metal, engraved with the image of an eagle. And there, just above the buttons, embroidered on the flap, were crossed swords—the symbol of a fighting man.

David remembered the moment Colonel Chamberlain had given it to him. It had been right before the charge at Gettysburg—July 2, 1863. He knew because he had been there. David had talked to Chamberlain, looked into his eyes, and felt the colonel's dirty hand in his.

He had later read all about Joshua Chamberlain. In the aftermath of the accident and his recovery, David had hours and weeks and months to do nothing but read and think and remember and plan. He had found himself especially curious about the young colonel. With the other Travelers, while surprising and exciting, he had at least a cultural familiarity.

But Chamberlain? David had never even heard of the man! And then to discover his extraordinary connection to the time in which David lived—and the almost inconceivable divergence of world events his single act that day in Pennsylvania had caused—well, it was just sometimes more than David could wrap his mind around.

Without opening his eyes, David shifted and reached out with his left hand. There, on the desk where it always was, rested a book—*Soul of the Lion*. It was a biography of Chamberlain and had a picture of him as an old man on the cover. David slid it from the desk and nestled it beside his leg.

He'd read the book many times. For years, David had carried it with him, and he practically knew it by heart.

Chamberlain had been a thirty-four-year-old schoolteacher during the fight, but when he got home, the people of Maine elected him governor in what today is still the highest percentage of winning votes in that state's history. Chamberlain served four terms, leaving office in order to use his time and money to write and teach.

Reading that Chamberlain originally studied to be a missionary, David thought many times, *Well, if the hand of God was on anybody, it was most surely on Joshua Lawrence Chamberlain.* The young colonel had personally shown him the bent and busted belt buckle—destroyed by a Confederate bullet—that had saved his life that day.

Years later, in a museum in Maine, David had read the letter—written to then Governor Chamberlain from a Rebel sharpshooter—that had recounted his peculiar experience in the battle. The sniper had drawn down on Chamberlain, knowing who he was by his uniform and manner, and had him in his sights two separate times—but he had not been able to pull the trigger. Even so long after the event, the Confederate soldier had expressed amazement at being unable to shoot, claiming that a "strange something" had stopped him.

"The hand of God," was how David explained it. He was certain that Joshua Chamberlain felt the same way.

In researching many books, talking to historians, confirming papers upon papers of military briefings still available from the Civil War, David had confirmed the fact that an astounding six different horses had been shot out from under Chamberlain, and still the officer had not been killed.

The hand of God.

David sighed and opened his eyes. He had hoped to fall asleep. It was easier to fall asleep in the chair and just wake up in the morning. It made him sad to go into the bedroom. Brushing his teeth, reading alone, turning out the light by himself. It was almost more than he could bear.

He put the book back on his desk where it belonged and situated the tobacco pouch on the leather writing pad. Smoothing it with his fingers, he sat back in his chair. Almost immediately, he leaned forward again. Vaguely aware that he had performed this ritual thousands of times, David carefully opened the right side of the tobacco pouch, then the left. Emptying its contents, he began to array them in order across his desk.

First was a small, crisply folded page from President Harry Truman. Titled *The Buck Stops Here*, the thirty-third president's handwritten commentary about the power of responsibility was placed to David's left.

Next was a tiny, bundled scroll that had been tightly wound, despite the absence of its original wooden rod. As he had done with the first item, David left it as it had been removed from the pouch. He didn't need to see it again. The words, the very placement of each ink scratch that denoted every single letter, had been burned into his memory. *I will seek wisdom.* David had read the scroll hundreds of times—maybe a thousand times—and he knew by heart every word King Solomon had written.

Third was Chamberlain's decision. A hastily scrawled-upon piece of paper, produced in bad light, it had been wadded up and carried for two months by the young colonel before he had known what to do with it—long before David had appeared during the roar of the battle. *I am a person of action.*

Then the parchment from Columbus, brittle but still in reasonable shape. *I have a decided heart.* David always smiled when he thought of Columbus. The explorer had seemed almost crazy to him, but the man's ability to focus on his objective and tune out unnecessary criticism had been a large part of changing David's financial life. From that point forward, anytime he met a young person who didn't quite fit—whose dreams irritated reasonable society—David always harkened back to his night in the crow's nest with a visionary.

Number five. David drew a deep breath and sang aloud. "La la la la la la." Years before, he had gotten in the habit of singing some off-key little nothing when he removed Anne Frank's pages. There were four of them, folded in half, and they were very small. The papers had been torn from her diary, and for a long time, David cried every time he brought them out. His singing was an unsuccessful diversion to the overwhelming emotion he felt toward the tiny girl and the irony of the words she had written for him: *Today I will choose to be happy.*

Once, on a European trip, David and Ellen had gone to

the museum in Amsterdam dedicated to Anne, the twelve-year-old girl who, with her parents and friends, hid from the Nazis in the annex of an apartment building. There she had kept a diary that was later published, astonishing the world.

That day, as they toured the tiny hiding place, David whispered to Ellen, pointing out the things *he* remembered—things he had seen when he had been there, with Anne Frank, on Thursday evening, October 28, 1943. Of course, Ellen didn't believe him. Why on earth would anyone in their right mind have believed him? David grinned at the memory and swiped at the tears flowing down his face. "La la la la la la la laaaa."

So he had waited until the tour ended and approached the museum manager. Quietly, he asked the man if he would remove Anne's diary from the glass case in the center of the room. There was no one there. It was closing time. David did not even want to touch it, he had said. He simply wanted to see it. The manager could stand with them, David had explained, and never take his hands off the book.

Of course, the man had refused. When David did not relent and began begging for just one moment with the diary, the manager actually threatened to call the police. Ellen had not understood and was horribly upset, but when David pulled out his wallet and began peeling off American one-hundred-dollar bills, she grew quiet. Ellen had never seen him this way.

David stopped when he had counted out two thousand dollars. The man looked briefly at the door, then at David.

Quickly brushing the money into a pile, he nervously shoved it into his pocket. Swiftly, the manager stepped to the glass case and, with a key from his pocket, unlocked the cover. Reaching inside, he gingerly removed the red-orange, cloth-bound book.

Glancing to the door, he said, "Hurry, please. What is it you want to see?"

"Just turn the pages for us, can you?" David answered. "One at a time."

As he did so, Ellen held her breath while David removed something from a plastic bag in his back pocket. Within moments, David ordered, "Stop. Stop right there."

The man did not move as David slowly placed four small, lined pages, one by one, into the diary. The torn edges, the ink, and the handwriting matched perfectly. "Thank you," David whispered to the manager as he removed the four fragments constituting the Fifth Decision from the tiny book. Gently, he led his stunned wife from the premises.

"La la la la la la la la la," David sang unevenly as he patted the little pages and situated them on the desk, just to the right of the parchment.

Wiping his eyes with his handkerchief, David inhaled deeply to gain control. "La la la la la la!" he said forcefully. "Today I will choose to be happy." In his speeches about the Seven Decisions for Success, he often expressed how unnatural this principle felt to him at first.

From the beginning, "choosing to *act* happy" long before

he felt anywhere near the mark was hard for David. But he knew—had seen the evidence proven beyond doubt many times—that *Today I will choose to be happy* was the single most powerful leadership tool that existed. And, oddly enough, it was the key to the financial fortune many people sought.

Anne Frank was important to David for another reason. As he researched her life and death and the murder of millions just like her, David came to believe that people could not be reminded enough about that moment in time. In his speeches and interviews, David stated again and again that America and Europe especially must never forget the atrocities that had been allowed.

David had studied history, and he knew the facts. Fewer than 10 percent of the German population had been *actively involved* in the Nazi rise to power. Fewer than 10 percent of the population of a modern, industrial nation had actually campaigned to give authority to a man who, only months before being elected, had been an army lieutenant.

David studied public statements and speeches. He pored over government documents, election archives, and legislative decisions. The evidence was overwhelming and available to anyone with the click of a computer key: Adolf Hitler had risen to power during a time of economic uncertainty in a nation of people desperate for identity and longing for better times.

This man of the common people—as Hitler had called himself—stood up, looked them in the eye, and lied. He promised more and better and new and different. He vowed rapid change and swift action. David studied the recorded words of every public address the Führer delivered. He assembled and recalculated numbers and lists of volunteers and voting archives. It had all been available. After all, the Third Reich maintained excellent records.

David saw for himself, from the vantage point of his own generation, fewer than 10 percent of the people of one nation had worked to bring about Hitler's "change." What David could never understand is how the remaining 90 percent—doctors and teachers and ministers and farmers—did . . . what? Stood by? Watched? It shocked and frightened him.

David knew that many of those people had turned their heads and, by not raising their voices, allowed the Holocaust to take place. Mothers and fathers closed their eyes and covered their ears and accepted their salaries, avoiding the truth that lingered over them like a serpent waiting to strike. And when the Nazis came for *their* children, it was too late.

Wiping his eyes with both hands, David sniffed loudly and coughed a bit, clearing his throat. Lincoln's decision—*I will greet each day with a forgiving spirit*—was not written on formal stationery. Examining it as he drew the paper from the tobacco pouch, David knew the sixteenth president had handwritten the powerful words while on the train to Gettysburg.

He smiled, remembering Lincoln's confusion that day when David had asked if he had written the Gettysburg Address on the train. After all, that had been the rumor for more than a century. "No," the president had replied. "My speech for this occasion today was written back in Washington. On the train," he said, handing David the Sixth Decision, "I was writing this for you."

David placed the single piece of paper beside the pages from Anne Frank and felt a chill run up his spine as he reached into the tobacco pouch for the last item. He had never gotten used to handling the Seventh Decision. It was a small scroll made of . . . well, exactly what, David had never been able to determine.

Having been presented to him by the archangel Gabriel, the scroll and the physical properties it exhibited were strange indeed. From the first moment he had touched it, David perceived a faint electrical charge that had never gone away or even diminished. Also still evident, David saw as he turned the scroll in his hands, was the original luminescence, an odd glow that he had noticed the moment Gabriel placed it in his hands. *I will persist without exception*—the final decision that bound the six others into a life-changing force—had been composed, David finally decided, on celestial paper.

Carefully depositing the precious scroll to the far right of the others, David leaned back in his chair and sighed deeply. At that moment, he missed Ellen more than ever. Their relationship had changed dramatically that day in the Anne Frank museum. David had always known that his wife *wanted* to believe his astonishing time travel had actually happened, but without real proof, he knew that the whole adventure was simply too fantastic to believe.

After the initial shock of seeing the evidence with her own eyes, Ellen left Amsterdam with a newfound respect for her husband. From that moment forward, they had become a team in every sense of the word. Virtually inseparable, David and Ellen never made an important decision, business or otherwise, without the knowledge and approval of the other. Their love for each other, while always evident, became boundless.

And now she was gone. David's life, having been so inexorably linked to his soul mate, was over. Of this fact, David was certain. While his mind acknowledged that Ellen would have wanted him to "persist without exception," his heart was broken in a million pieces, and he could not find a way to begin again.

Eighteen months earlier, encouraged by Ellen, David had started writing, but the manuscript about which she had been so excited lay on a chair in the corner of his office, untouched since she had passed away.

A sob escaped David's mouth as his tears began to flow freely. Over the months since his wife's sudden death, David had dismissed fleeting thoughts of suicide, knowing that desperate act would help no one, dishonor Ellen's memory, and very likely harm the financial legacy he had created for charitable organizations. On the other hand, he didn't understand why he had been left alone.

Overwhelmed by grief, David reached for the tobacco pouch and the Seven Decisions and drew them into a pile. Placing his arms around the items and his head on top of his arms, he wept in great, agonizing sobs.

CHAPTER 2

"Hello, David Ponder," Gabriel said. "You have aged." David had almost fallen from his chair when he looked up and saw the archangel, but he recovered quickly. "Hello, Gabriel," he responded. "I see you haven't gained any tact since we last met."

Gabriel cocked his head. "Tact is a human trait," he stated, "needed only by those who hesitate to tell the truth."

Though his legs were shaky at the sight of his unexpected visitor, David somehow managed to stand. Vaguely aware that he had no idea about etiquette or any specific protocol required to greet a heavenly guest, David did not attempt to shake hands or even touch the archangel. He did, however, look upon him in awe.

In contrast to his own changes that Gabriel had mentioned, David saw that the archangel's physical appearance was exactly as he'd remembered. He was well over six feet tall and muscular, with clear blue eyes and relatively short, curly blond hair that brushed his ears and eyebrows.

The archangel's robe had a disconcerting way of appearing common and otherworldly at the same time. Its cut was traditional—mere layers of cloth—but its hue was jaw-dropping. David had once described Gabriel's robe to Ellen by saying,

"The color is whiter than white. It is almost a shade of *light*." Indeed, the fabric radiated a luminescence that was virtually indescribable.

Then, of course, there were his wings. Although massive when extended, at rest Gabriel's supernatural appendages tucked neatly behind him, sometimes completely hidden by the moving folds of his robe. They were bright white—of the same shade as the robe—but dusted with deep gold on the tip of every feather. David could not help staring in hopes of catching a better look, for it was when Gabriel moved that the wings were more easily seen. Flexing and rippling, they seemed to have a life of their own.

"I'm glad to see you again, Gabriel," David said. "Or maybe I am just relieved."

Gabriel looked evenly at the older man. "Why might you be relieved to see me, David Ponder?"

Making his way around the desk, David tried to explain. "Well . . . I assume your being here must mean that my life is over. Will I be able to see Ellen soon?"

Gabriel crossed his arms. With only a hint of a smile, he said, "You made the same erroneous assumption the first time we met."

"What do you mean?" David asked, startled.

"You presume that my arrival coincides with your demise. But again I must declare that you are far from dead, David Ponder."

"Oh," David sighed, not knowing whether to be relieved or disappointed. "But I thought—"

"And before you ask," the archangel interrupted, "the answer is no. You are not dreaming either."

"Then why are you here?" David asked simply.

"I am here to present myself as your guide and facilitator for the upcoming summit conference."

David shook his head quickly as if to clear the cobwebs from his brain. "Summit conference . . . what? Gabriel, am I supposed to know what you are talking about?"

Allowing a bit of impatience to show, the archangel flexed his wings slightly and responded, "Our time is short, David Ponder. Obviously, the lack of cognitive intelligence between us will not allow me to simply retrieve you and depart. Therefore, I am at your disposal for several minutes before we must go. Feel at ease to ask your questions."

David snorted. "Feel at ease, huh? I'm not sure anybody ever feels at ease around you. You and the other archangel."

"Michael."

"Yes, Michael," David said. "In the Bible, every time one of you guys appears, you're always telling folks, 'Fear not!' or 'Don't be afraid!' So . . . ," he explained with a grin, "don't tell *me* to feel at ease. I think you already know how nervous folks are when you show up."

At that moment, David almost laughed out loud. He had gotten used to speaking his mind and having folks accept it with good humor simply because he was an older man. But the look on Gabriel's face was priceless. David wondered if any human had ever talked to him that way.

In addition, David was certain he was among the few on earth to actually see the archangel twice. The first time they'd met, it had been in "the place that never was"—a depository of lost dreams and unfinished prayers. Then David had been so overwhelmed by everything he was experiencing, he'd paid little attention to how Gabriel acted toward him. Actually, he wasn't certain the subject of an archangel's personality was relevant in *any* event, but he was curious about him.

When Gabriel spoke, he did so evenly, and his eyes seemed to gather every detail. There was a trace of superiority in his manner that David did not find objectionable. In fact, Gabriel's comment about tact and honesty was telling.

What would it be like, David wondered, to live "in truth" every day, to speak and hear and think only the truth every moment? *It'll never happen on this planet,* David mused; *that's for sure. Maybe that's why Gabriel seems impatient.* It would be hard, he finally decided, to filter every word or nuance, turning it over in your mind, on guard to avoid the tiniest deception.

"So," David began, "you said that there is an upcoming summit conference. Why don't you start there?"

"Let me begin with *why* the summit is being allowed," Gabriel stated coolly.

David caught something in the archangel's bearing—a warning, perhaps—and furrowed his brow. "All right," he said softly.

With a serious nod, Gabriel began. "You are at a turning point," he said. "You—the human race—are balanced on a precipice, and He is not pleased. Just as Amos once pled for the nation of Israel, so now the Travelers are being convened with an opportunity to avoid what seems to me, the inevitable."

David blinked. "Wow," he said. "And whoa. Hold on. I had some questions before, but you just raised a whole load of new ones. The Travelers are being convened? What Travelers? And where?"

"Every Traveler will attend the summit. I will facilitate the meeting. We will not be here." Gabriel made the last statement and glanced around curiously, as if he were just noticing his surroundings.

David had been leaning against his desk. Standing straight, he moved closer to Gabriel and asked, "You said 'every Traveler.' How many Travelers are there?"

"Many," the archangel answered simply.

"Okay. Well, I guess I understand that humanity is in a bad place—'balanced on a precipice,' I think is how you put it—so what will happen if the Travelers don't . . . well, I don't even know what we're supposed to do!"

"There have been times in the history of your planet, David Ponder, when He has elected to . . . ah . . . how should I say this to a human?" Smiling suddenly, Gabriel thought of the term for which he had been grasping, and continued. ". . . when He has elected to start over."

David's eyebrows rose. "What do you mean?"

The expression on Gabriel's face was as if he had been

rebuked for speaking harshly to a dense child. "I'm sorry," he said. "I thought that was plain enough without delving into excessive details. Allow me to use a different phrase. There have been times in the history of your civilization when He has elected to start over, begin afresh, create anew . . ."

"I understood what you meant, Gabriel," David inserted. "I was asking, what might happen?"

Readjusting his wings, Gabriel stated, "Surely you know that I do not make those specific decisions. Neither do I speculate on what might be. However, if one gazed into the past, seeking historical context, the most recent reorganization would have been the Flood."

David was taken aback. "The Flood? You mean Noah and the ark? That actually happened? I always assumed it was a . . . you know . . . a *story*, a parable. Or if it really occurred, that it was a regional event."

There was an uncomfortable pause before Gabriel spoke. When he did, he said, "David Ponder, I have often been amazed by the human tendency to ignore the obvious and rewrite history into accounts more palatable or easier to understand.

"In addition to the abundant geological evidence, your own civilization records more than five hundred different cultures with separate and distinct accounts of a great flood," Gabriel noted. "In every instance—though these writers and storytellers were divided by continents and languages and mountains and seas—the details of the event they recorded remained the same. Forty days, forty nights. A deluge that was survived only by a man and his family in a vast ship that had been constructed specifically to protect thousands of pairs of animals from the water, and a dove released to find dry land as that water receded."

Gazing steadily into David's eyes, Gabriel said, "You call him Noah. In Sumeria, he was called Ziusudra. In Babylon, Uta-Napishtim. The Greeks said his name was Deucalion. In Armenia, he was Xisuthrus. On the continent of India, they called him Menue—"

"Do you know them all?" David interrupted.

"Of course," Gabriel replied.

Nodding, David echoed the answer, "Of course." Taking a deep breath, he returned to the subject of the summit. "So we are to gather—all of us, all the Travelers—and do what?"

"Together, you will convene with the opportunity to examine the accumulated wisdom of the past in order to determine your future. Or if there is even to be a future on this earth—"

David's mouth was agape. He couldn't believe what he was hearing. Interrupting, he said, "I don't understand . . ."

"Were it my choice, David Ponder," Gabriel said calmly, "I might have turned my back on you years ago. But He still has hope, though His heart is heavy and patience decidedly thin."

Gabriel looked closely at David as if deciding whether to reveal more. "The fact," he finally said, "is that humanity is sinking of its own accord."

"What do you mean?" David asked.

"Isn't it obvious?" Gabriel shot back. "For many years, you have progressively turned away from the real truth and in its stead have attempted to create your own version of a 'truth' that your intellect can comprehend. In so doing, you have become increasingly hungry for the attributes of destruction— an unquenchable thirst for riches, a disdain for your fellow man, and power for its own sake."

"So what you mean by 'humanity is sinking of its own accord—,'" David began.

Gabriel finished the thought. "What I mean is that *this time*, quite simply, you are providing your own flood. Certainly you are aware that some of the so-called progress you have pursued now enables you to destroy all life on this planet in several different ways, many times over, and with varying choices of speed. You don't need *Him* to make it rain."

Stunned, David asked, "Is there anything that can be done?"

"Of course," Gabriel responded. "That is the very reason for the gathering of Travelers. But you must be aware of the truth in regard to your question: you have *always* had a choice. Since the very beginning of time, you have always possessed the gift and power of free will. Individually and collectively, every human's ultimate destination is a matter of choice— acceptance or rejection, yes or no, reward or punishment, life or death.

"If this council of Travelers is to succeed in its quest, you must seek to rediscover the path that has been abandoned. You must attempt to relight the darkness that has been allowed to overtake you. You must once again fight with the weapons of wisdom and persuasion to reclaim the authority that has been yielded."

David's mind worked furiously to fathom the information he was being given. "Is there a specific question we must answer?" he asked.

"Yes," Gabriel replied, "and when the assembly is gathered, that question will be put to you. You will also be given specific rules and a constraint of time within which the question must be answered."

"A constraint of time?" David blurted. "This seems so important that I can't imagine a limit—"

"It is no wonder you try His patience, David Ponder," the archangel scoffed. "A few moments ago, you hoped your time on earth was at an end. Now you argue about time's restriction."

"I'm sorry," David murmured. "You're right, of course. It isn't as if we haven't been given time already."

Without acknowledging that statement, Gabriel asked, "Do you have any more questions?"

"No," David said. "I suppose I will find out anything else there is to know when we get to . . . well, when we get to wherever it is we are going." Taking a deep breath and attempting to smile, he added, "It calms me a bit to know that you are leading this meeting."

Gabriel extended his right wing just a bit and, with his

hand, brushed something from it. "On the contrary, David Ponder," he said, still looking at his wing. "I merely stated that I would facilitate the summit. I am not the leader of this quest. My charge is to establish guidelines for the search, mark the boundary of time available for discussion, and formally issue the question the Travelers must answer."

"Oh," David said, a bit surprised. "Is there to be a leader? I mean, has a leader already been chosen?"

"Yes," Gabriel replied as he once again gazed around the room.

David raised his eyebrows and leaned forward, waiting expectantly, though from experience he knew that the archangel pointedly refused to answer even an obvious question until the question was actually asked.

"Okay," David prompted, trying not to let his impatience show, "who is the person who will lead this summit for the Travelers?"

With that question, Gabriel turned his full attention to David and said simply, "You."

David paused as his mouth dropped open. He closed it and grinned. Then, just as quickly, he frowned deeply, finally stammering, "Me? You have got to be joking!"

Not uttering a sound or even blinking, Gabriel remained motionless, looking at the seventy-four-year-old man before him, who seemed about to have a heart attack.

David hesitated a moment, decided Gabriel wasn't going to speak, and turned his back on the archangel with his hands on his hips. Immediately, he spun around and started again. "Me? Oh come on! If this whole thing hadn't happened to me before, I wouldn't even believe it now. I'd just crawl into bed and wait to wake up. But here you are again, and now you're telling me that . . ." David pulled up short and scowled. "Me?" he said again. "Holy mother of God!"

Gabriel raised an eyebrow.

Hastily, David apologized. "I'm sorry. I didn't mean that like it sounded. I'm just . . . Me?"

"Yes, David Ponder," Gabriel said calmly, "you."

Taking a deep breath and walking a quick circle around his desk, David attempted to match the archangel's demeanor.

"Listen, Gabriel . . ." Noticing the eyebrow rising again, David started over. "I mean, *please* listen to me, Gabriel. I accept that everything you tell me is true. Okay. That means—at least, I am assuming that means—that every person in history who has ever been a Traveler will be at this summit conference."

Gabriel nodded.

Striving to keep his wits about him and proceed with his line of reasoning, David rubbed his suddenly clammy hands on his pants legs and continued. "Okay. Okay," he said, struggling to stay with his line of thought as his mind whirled out of control, "if every Traveler who ever existed is present at this conference, that means that for sure Christopher Columbus will be there. Harry Truman. Abraham Lincoln?"

Again Gabriel nodded.

"And holy . . . King Solomon? Gabriel! He was the wisest

man in the history of the world! And I'm supposed to lead this meeting? Why me?!"

Unfazed by the outburst and waiting a moment to ensure that David was finished, Gabriel answered evenly. "David Ponder, you have been chosen to lead this forum for three reasons.

"First, you are the only Traveler currently living in earth's present time period. Thus, theoretically, the results of this assembly should matter more to you.

"Second, you have been judged extremely effective in utilizing the wisdom you gathered as a Traveler.

"Last—and perhaps most important—you are the only Traveler who was ever chosen to represent the common man."

David frowned. "I'm not sure I understand," he said.

For the first time since his arrival, Gabriel moved from where he had been standing. He walked to a position behind the desk and motioned for David to stand next to him. Touching the tobacco pouch, then each of the Seven Decisions in turn, Gabriel began to explain. "Do you remember, David Ponder, when we first met, I informed you of your significance in the long history of Travelers?" The archangel paused and looked carefully into David's eyes, waiting for an answer.

"Yes, I *do* remember," David responded. "I've thought about what you told me many times. You said that I was the last Traveler. You said that after me, there would not be another."

"That is correct," Gabriel said. "What you did not know at

that time is that you were deemed ordinary. All Travelers who preceded you were either already remarkable human specimens or they had greatness in their sights.

"You, on the other hand, were an ideal example of the human race. You were uncertain of your life's purpose, inconsistent in your actions and attitudes, and angry about it all. At the instant of your life's most critical crossroad, you were chosen to represent your fellow man. You were given the gift of a travel through the ages.

"In the years that followed, your search for wisdom continued. And though, like all humans, your road was peppered with failure, you prudently used even your failures to advance wisdom's cause. And you did this not only for yourself, but also for others. You have generously shared what you have learned and what you have become.

"Because of what you have accomplished and who you have become, David Ponder, you are now acknowledged— even by the other Travelers—as the greatest of them all."

David was thunderstruck. "There's no way," he stammered. "I can't believe that the other Travelers even know who I am. And that they consider me the . . . well, I can't even say it! That's just not possible!"

Placing his hands on David's shoulders, Gabriel said, "I speak only the truth, David Ponder. It is for this reason alone that the last Traveler has been chosen to lead the final summit."

David couldn't breathe, but he didn't know what he would

have done with the breath anyway. He had nothing left to say. Finally, able to speak at last, David said simply, "Okay." Then, "Well, Gabriel, when do we leave?"

Removing his hands from David's shoulders, the archangel reached behind the older man and clasped his waist tightly. With his left wing, Gabriel covered David from the back of his head to his lower legs as he raised the right wing slowly above them. In one mighty stroke, Gabriel drew his wing suddenly to the floor, thrusting them up like a rocket, through the ceiling and into the night sky. The archangel, with his head tucked closely to David's, whispered into his ear, "Right now."

CHAPTER 3

David remembered a sensation of surging upward and seeing bursting streaks of colored light before he passed out. As he began to regain consciousness, he found himself unable to move or even open his eyes, but he was intensely aware of extreme speed and a sound like none he had ever heard. And it was not a pleasant sound, resonating with a low rumble like the aftershock of an explosion mixed with the shrill high-end whine of a jet engine.

Though nauseated by the noise and acceleration, David was relieved to feel Gabriel's arms still locked around him. Try as he might, however, he could not think clearly.

Colorful dreams or visions battered their way into his mind, materializing suddenly and disappearing with the speed of light. He saw his first house. Then Jenny, his daughter, as a toddler taking her first steps . . . King Solomon's throne room . . . the Dodge Colt he had wrecked before his first travel, his parents as a young couple . . . his last kiss with Ellen as she left for Austin, followed inexplicably by jumbled scenes from their wedding and her funeral.

As if he were high above the action, David witnessed Chamberlain's charge at Gettysburg. He watched as his shaky hand signed the bankruptcy papers, and he saw himself strolling Big Reef Beach on Peter Island. David watched in horror as Lincoln shifted in his chair in the booth at Ford's Theatre, a dark figure behind him, reaching out . . .

And once again he saw Ellen, beautiful Ellen, in the blue dress he liked so much. "Honey," she said, extending her hand to touch him, but oddly, at the same time, drifting up and away, "I am depending on you. I am depending on you. I am depending on you . . ."

"David Ponder," Gabriel said suddenly, "we have arrived."

Opening his eyes, David's mind cleared. He was, he noted, already seated at the head of a rectangular table with chairs set on a fine, purple linen rug. Taking a quick glance around, David could not see anything else nearby—not even walls.

The floor, which continued into the darkness beyond the table, was hardwood and had been polished to a high finish. Immediately, David decided that there had never been a floor to equal this one. The planks were enormous, obviously cut from large trees. Every grain of the burnished timber was distinct, and the seams between the massive slats were filled with . . . *Well, if it isn't real gold*, David thought, *it certainly looks like gold.*

Aware of a glass in his hand, David saw that it contained a clear liquid. Raising it to Gabriel, he asked, "Water?"

With an amused expression, the archangel answered, "Of course," and motioned for his guest to drink.

David did so immediately. Returning the glass to the table, he stood and practically fell back into the chair, looking at his host with alarm.

"*Dizziness* is the word I believe you use for that sensation," Gabriel explained matter-of-factly. "It will pass momentarily." The archangel moved behind David, causing him to twist to his right in the chair. "I will leave you now for a short time," he said. "Rest if you wish."

"When will I meet the others?" David asked. "When will we begin?"

"Soon," Gabriel answered and turned, walking directly away from the head of the table toward a magnificent door that illuminated as he approached. The door was made entirely of beautiful stone—marble or granite, David assumed—and shimmered with veins of green and silver and white. He had never seen anything like it and was awed, but not surprised, when the archangel simply laid his palm on the door and it opened. Gabriel's hand came to rest where a handle or knob might otherwise have been situated, but the stone appeared almost weightless as it smoothly swung away from the room.

Intense, white light radiated from the other side as the door opened, causing David to shield his eyes with a hand. Gabriel, however, simply walked through the doorway and turned back toward David. That particular visual perspective of the archangel's outline, surrounded by light, was a vision David wanted to remember forever. It was a sight that took his breath away.

Gabriel was still for a moment before repeating his last word. "Soon," he said, and the massive door slowly closed.

Intrigued with his surroundings, David cautiously got to his feet, grateful that his equilibrium had returned. He was not in the least bit afraid and chuckled as he acknowledged that fact to himself. On the other hand, David's excitement level was at an all-time high. He was eager, but somewhat nervous, to meet the other participants. And while he still wasn't fully confident about his own ability to contribute, much less *lead*, David felt certain that the wisdom these Travelers brought to the table would quickly solve whatever question Gabriel might ask.

That was another thing David was curious about: what *was* the question? His mind did somersaults around the idea. *I have a question about a question*, David thought, amused with himself, *and I don't even know the question!*

Eager to explore his surroundings and assuming it was permissible to do so, David walked first to the door Gabriel had used. There was, he noted, no other choice. It was the only door in the room. The door was shrouded in darkness, but the first step David took in its direction seemed to turn on a light. David looked up and was not surprised to find that he could not locate the source of the light. It didn't seem to emanate from any particular place. The light was simply there.

David smiled as he neared the door and the light became brighter. It was exactly the same kind of light that had seemed so incredible to him years ago, in "the place that never was," when he had first encountered Gabriel.

The door was as large as David had first thought, maybe larger. It was framed in rich, dark wood that had been carved into strong shapes with soft edges. The frame was beautiful, but as David looked closely, he knew there was no way on earth that any wooden frame—even one that had been reinforced—could support the gigantic stone door. *That's exactly right*, David thought to himself, as he took one last look and turned again toward the room. *No way on earth . . .*

After a few steps, David paused between the table and the door. A quick glance behind him was all it took to see that the light on the door had dimmed. Again, he shook his head in wonder and tried to concentrate on what lay before him.

The table, like everything else he had seen, was one of a kind. It was a simple yet fascinating design that would have been equally at home in a palace or a workshop. It had been constructed, David saw at once, without nails. Wooden pegs and carved grooves fit together perfectly in a pattern that not only attached the table legs but joined the pieces of wood forming the top.

It had been sanded, rubbed, and oiled by hand, David knew, and as he ran his fingers along the table's edge, he also saw the elegant beveling that had been done by someone with patience and care. *No machine ever touched this table*, David mused.

The chairs had been created to match and were as

beautiful and unpretentious as the table. Three sat along each side. One end had been left empty, making the head of the table a foregone conclusion, even though that particular chair was no larger than the others and all seven were cushioned similarly. David touched the top of one of the chair backs, admiring the precise woodwork. Each had been hand carved, duplicating the table's edge.

After taking the time to appreciate the craftsmanship, David moved to sit at the table. He had no desire to explore the darkness beyond what he could see and thought he might take a moment to gather his wits. Disregarding the place he had initially occupied, David carried his glass of water beyond that chair, passed another seat, and chose the next position down—the middle chair on the left side.

David took a sip from the water glass and closed his eyes. Breathing deeply, he tried to clear his mind but found it difficult to ignore his current location, which was . . . where? He didn't know, but smiled as he thought he might get close with a couple of guesses. *How much time has passed since Gabriel appeared in my office?* David wondered. *Fifteen minutes? Fifteen hours?* He wasn't sure.

When he opened his eyes a few moments later, he sensed immediately that something had changed. At first, David was uncertain about exactly what that might be, but he quickly determined that it was the light. The light in the room was brighter. And the circle of light around the table had broadened. No, he decided, it was *broadening.* As David watched, ever so slowly, the light inched away from him on all sides, creating an ever-widening circle.

At about twenty feet from the table, as if illuminated from the side, but again with no source, upright objects began to appear. David turned to look behind himself. To the left, right—everywhere he looked—what appeared to be sticks or poles were slowly being revealed in the expanding circle of light.

He didn't leave the chair. David didn't move at all except to occasionally glance around. Fascinated by what he was watching, he worried that if he did move, the light might stop. So he waited. *Sticks? Poles? What is this?* David wondered. Then, all at once, he knew.

When the light revealed the vertically placed sticks to the height of about eighteen inches, a "top" came into view. Another inch or two of light and David recognized fabric that looked like . . . well, the fabric looked like the very cushion upon which he was sitting. When the seat backs came into sight, David realized that he was surrounded with chairs— chairs identical to the ones around the table.

It took some time, but the circle of light gradually revealed another row of chairs behind the first. They were raised at least eighteen inches higher than the first row. A ring of chairs circled by a loftier ring of chairs. There were several areas of steps or stairs situated between the levels.

The area being illuminated continued to increase until David could clearly see four rows, each higher than the one before it. Though the light dimmed considerably after the fourth row, there were quite obviously more seats beyond those he was able to distinguish from his position at the table. David was able to make out a fifth and sixth row, but behind those, he had no idea how high they went, and in any case, the light was no longer moving.

Unexpectedly, David smelled smoke. Frowning, he looked around. It was cigar smoke. David recognized the aroma immediately. He loved cigars but had sworn them off years ago for Ellen. What was a fragrance to him had been a fetid stench to her. With a bit of poking and prodding, David had finally admitted that Ellen's allergies trumped his desire for burning leaves, and from the day he had surrendered, he never smoked another cigar. Even when he was alone.

Now that acrid bouquet was beckoning him again. Turning to his left, David saw a wisp of smoke drift against the shadowy background behind him. Attempting to follow the trail with his eyes, David peered into the darkness and located its source. There, at about seven o'clock behind him on row six, stood . . . someone.

That someone was dressed in black, making it difficult to discern, but when the cigar was puffed, its fiery red glow allowed David to catch a glimpse of a pale, balding old man's face, framed by thin strands of snow-white hair. And a hat. A black one.

The man loudly cleared his throat. David stared into the darkness, trying to see what he obviously could not. Moving forward, the man came down two steps. David saw his legs and a walking cane that was as black as the man's pants. "Well, well," the man said in a raspy voice with a thick British accent. "If you are who I think you are, it is an honor to make your acquaintance, sir."

"Thank you. It's nice to meet you as well," David responded without a clue to the identity of the person with whom he was suddenly chatting, for he still could not clearly see the man's face. Nonetheless, he stood and strode forward as the man moved unsteadily toward another step.

Working his way down several more stairs, the old man—the chubby old man, David could now see—wore a black derby, pushed hard onto his head. His cane probed forward as he made a very deliberate descent, purposefully concentrating on every step. Of course, with his head down, the hat continued to obscure his face. Which was why, though the man was now fully in the light, David had yet to get a good look at him.

Finally, the old man reached the floor and tucked the cane under his arm. Removing the cigar from his mouth, he shoved his right hand forward to shake. With a great smile, he thrust his face out over his shoulders and roared, "Ponder! Good man!"

It was Winston Churchill.

A shiver ran through David's body. It was happening again. He was older now and more prepared for the shock of meeting someone from another place and time, but it was still incredible. Here was the man whom he had read about and seen on newsreels. Here . . . in the flesh. David grinned and pumped Churchill's hand vigorously.

"You are the hero of the moment, I understand," Churchill said cheerily as he moved toward the table.

"I'm sorry?" David responded, sounding confused.

"Oh, come now," Churchill chuckled. "I know all about the great David Ponder. I've been briefed, as we used to say at 10 Downing. Word is, you're in the hot seat."

"I suppose that's true," David said slowly. "Gabriel . . . ," he started to say, then interjected, "You've met Gabriel?"

The great man's eyebrows rose. "Indeed."

"Gabriel said that because I am the only Traveler living in the . . . ah . . . present time . . ." Flustered, David stopped again. "But I suppose it's not the present time for you."

"Certainly, it is the present time for me as well," Churchill said, nodding. "Difference is, nowadays, I do a lot more watching and a bit less *doing* from my vantage point."

David wanted to ask the former British prime minister exactly what that vantage point was but decided to save the question for later. Instead, he attempted to get back on track. "So anyway, Gabriel told me that because I was currently living on earth," David said, noting to himself that this conversation was already the craziest he'd ever had in his life (and that was saying something), "that I would be the . . . well, as you put it . . . the one in the hot seat."

"You are the leader of our little gathering," Churchill said as he chose the chair to the right of David's and sat down. "Go on now; you can say it. 'I am the leader.' Say it."

"I'd rather not," David replied.

"Say it, old son!" Churchill demanded sternly. He held his scowling pose for a moment and dissolved into laughter. "Ha!" he exclaimed loudly. "I was only joking, of course, but the look on your face was priceless." Taking a deep breath, Churchill visibly relaxed. "Call me Winston."

"Really? All right. If you're sure," David said cautiously. He didn't know what to make of Churchill. The man wasn't what he had expected. *Then again,* he had to remind himself, *who expected to see Winston Churchill in the first place?*

"Yes, I am sure," he said, closing the matter. "Sit down. May I address you as David?"

"Yes, please," David agreed as he sat down in the same chair he had previously occupied.

"Well then, David," Winston began, "Are we indoors or out?"

"Excuse me?"

"Indoors or out, man?" Churchill barked. "My hat!"

David's line of sight rose from the prime minister's rheumy brown eyes past the white thatch of wild eyebrows to see that he was still wearing his hat.

Churchill roughly grabbed the derby and tossed it onto the table, rubbing the top of his head with a hand. Peering upward, he remarked, "Inside or outside? There doesn't seem to be an answer to that here. A decent man doesn't wear a hat indoors. Is it too much to ask to know whether one is indoors or out?" He paused only for a second.

With his chin jutted out, Churchill glared up again. "And where is that light coming from?"

David laughed out loud.

"I mean it!" Winston said, trying to suppress a grin. "No wind either. Have you noticed that? Where's the wind?" He stood up and shoved his head forward as David had seen him do when he introduced himself.

To no one in particular, Winston said, "I think we need a good thunderstorm every now and then. Some lightning. A lot of wind." His bottom lip was poked out, and David saw the old man steal a glance at him from the corner of his eye. "Do this place some good, it would. Keep everyone alert. Nothing like a good storm, I say, to clean the place up a bit."

David looked around. "It all seems pretty clean to me," he said with a smile, fairly certain that Winston was acting grumpy because he enjoyed it.

"Yes, it does," Churchill agreed as if he were disappointed and settled back into his chair. "Cigar?" he asked, reaching into his pocket and drawing out a fresh one.

Why not? David thought. *I am going to smoke a cigar with Winston Churchill.* "Absolutely," he said to the prime minister as he reached for the offering. "Thank you."

Churchill lit the cigar for him, a simple act that delighted David, and the two men began to lighten their mood. "I've followed your career since your travel, you know," Winston said.

David was surprised. "No," he said, "I didn't know. I really had no idea that kind of thing was done."

"Well . . .," Winston said, drawing out the word and gesturing with his cigar, "sometimes it is and sometimes it isn't." He squinted. "But I was especially interested in you. First, because of Lincoln. That was your sixth stop, if I remember correctly. I envied you that."

David tilted his head.

"Yes," Churchill continued, "I admit it. I did. Still might, actually." He scowled furiously, making David laugh, and just as quickly picked up his relaxed narrative. "I am—have always been—an unabashed Lincoln admirer. Read about him as a youngster. Love the man. Everything about him. And he was ugly. Like me. What better encouragement for a young politician, eh?" He and David laughed heartily.

Catching his breath, Winston continued with the cigar clamped tightly in the side of his mouth. "In any case, when I got word that a Traveler was about to meet with the old boy, I knew I couldn't miss it."

"You watched us?"

"Yes . . . yes! We don't see everything, of course, but Travelers who have 'slipped the surly bonds of Earth'—that, by the way, is a phrase I borrowed from another one of us—those of us who have passed on are allowed a certain . . . mmm . . . latitude, if you will." Churchill stopped and puffed the cigar furiously. "Where was I?"

David grinned. "You watched me with Abraham Lincoln."

"Yes! Hmm . . . Well, I became interested in you. Lincoln discussing forgiveness. You . . . going to church every week *because of the principle* of forgiveness, yet living your life as if you'd never heard of the concept!" Churchill banged his hand on the table, making David jump, but he nodded in agreement because it was true.

"So I was curious," Churchill went on. "And I asked myself, 'How will this young man respond?'" Leaning toward David, he added, "And you were a young man then." He fell back in his chair, fingers drumming on the table. David had never seen a person sitting down who seemed to be in such constant motion.

Churchill cleared his throat and continued. "I kept watching. Saw you with Gabriel in 'the place that never was.' He took me there, too, by the way. Dreadful place. Did me a lot of good, though, as I am certain it did you." He waited for David to nod, and when he'd gotten the reaction he was waiting for, he talked on.

"Very curious. Yes. Of course, I wondered what you'd do with the Seven Decisions. All the Travelers receive them, you know, in one form or another . . ."

"I didn't know," David said.

"Yes. Yes. So I was justifiably proud of your success and generosity when you got things moving upon your return to your own time. It's a bit of a fraternity, see, and we can be somewhat puffed up about each other. That being said, it is what we expect after all."

David tilted his head and, without saying anything, conveyed to the older gentleman that he didn't quite understand.

"It is expected!" Churchill repeated in a loud voice. "For God's own sake, man! You have the Seven Decisions for bloody Success right in your hands. All you must do is move! So we anticipate the success of a Traveler!"

Winston puffed hard on the cigar until regaining a calmer demeanor then said, "Yes. Your success was virtually preordained. Therefore, I was proud, but not surprised. My curiosity about you, however—and the curiosity of your fellow Travelers—was piqued when you lost it all."

"Yes," David said wryly, "my curiosity was piqued at that point as well."

"Ha!" Winston exclaimed. "Well put. Consequently, I was simply riveted by your comeback! Marvelous, actually. And here we all thought the Old Boy," Churchill pointed up with his finger, "had made a mistake. Ha again! Should have known better. You put us in our places. Bunch of Doubting Thomases we are—" Suddenly, he stopped in the middle of his thought and asked, "Have you met Thomas? He's here, you know," and immediately got back on course. "In any event, as a result of your greater success the next time around, my own accomplishments became a subject of discussion."

"Why was that?" David questioned.

"Because," Churchill said slowly as if talking to a dull pupil, "I was a 'second act man' myself!"

David smiled. "Okay, tell me what a 'second act man' is."

"Certainly," Winston nodded. "A 'second act man' is a term I coined myself. It describes perfectly a person—gentleman or lady—who has succeeded modestly or even greatly during the 'first act' of their life, only to suffer some tragedy during the intermission."

"Go on," David prodded.

Shifting in his chair, Churchill took his cigar out of his mouth and used it for emphasis. "Now, most folks—those who are only 'first act people'—spend the rest of their lives in a slow decline, thinking and talking about what was and what might have been. Very sad." He paused a moment, then shoved the cigar back in his mouth and puffed it to life again. "I say, 'Very sad.' Ha! Very sad for *them*!"

"But not for you?" David urged with a hint of a smile. He thought he knew where this was going.

"Of course not for me!" Churchill bellowed. "I was a Traveler. I knew the truth about my situation. The tragedy in man's life is not that he quits; the real tragedy is that he almost wins but never begins his second act! Strong people are sometimes allowed a taste of success—a sip of the good stuff—to whet their appetite for the long haul.

"But there is more to learn . . . more to become. Therefore, after the first act, some of us are given the gift of a vacation in the Valley of the Shadow of Death. There, in that Valley—where all of life's fertilizer seems to have leaked into a single spot—is where we become more. In the Valley we are allowed to think and brood. We experience loneliness and gain humility. We learn to focus our thoughts on others and not weep for ourselves.

"Then and only then do we gain glorious perspective. And as one Traveler put it, perspective brings calm. Calm leads to clear thinking. Clear thinking yields ideas. And from ideas, we get answers."

"Then the second act begins," David said quietly.

"Yes," Churchill agreed gruffly, moving in his chair a bit as if to shake off the suddenly somber mood. "Yes. Then the second act begins. And the second act makes the first look like so much chicken feed. We are allowed to take the memory of success—the certainty of knowing what can be done—add to it the fertilizer of wisdom and experience and fresh ideas and . . . Well, you are living proof of what happens.

"Or what is supposed to happen. It's disgraceful, you know, when it goes the other way." The cigar came out of his mouth again, and he was using it as a pointer. "I've seen many a man or woman having experienced the encouragement of success, given the benefit of time in the shadows, only to watch them simply refuse to come out of the Valley! Shocking! And none more surprised than the Almighty Himself! I know! I've been there. Seen Him upset about it. It's a terrible thing."

Churchill shoved the cigar back into his mouth and leaned back. He drew on it a few times, but the cigar had gone out. Reaching into his coat pocket, he pulled out an old Zippo lighter and refreshed the flame. Snapping it closed, he said, "Love this piece. Wouldn't trade it for the moon. One of your boys gave it to me." He passed the lighter to David, who looked at it admiringly.

"I visited an air base at the beginning of the fight. One of your boys came from Baltimore, Maryland, to train our pilots. His name was Tyler Mason. He was on loan to the RAF. Young fellow gave it to me and said he was going home the next day. Said he wouldn't dare smoke at home. Said his wife—Helen, he told me her name was; funny I never forgot it—wouldn't let him smoke." Churchill smiled. "I called him a sissy, and he laughed."

Churchill got a faraway look and said, "He never got home to that wife. Captain Tyler Mason. Killed in a Luftwaffe bombing raid thirty minutes after I left." He paused and reached for the lighter, placing it back into his pocket. David was quiet but watched him closely. "Yes. They were after me. Nazi intelligence had somehow pinpointed my location . . ." His voice trailed off. "I never called his wife. Never wrote either. Too busy . . . or something."

"I'm sure she's fine now, wherever she is," David said.

"Yes. Surely she is," Winston agreed and took a deep breath. "How did I get on that subject? Oh. The lighter." He frowned momentarily but recovered, saying, "I was congratulating you on your 'second act.' Brilliant."

"Thank you," David murmured.

"Second acts can be quite stunning." Winston stuck out his chin and declared, "Mine was, of course," which caused David to smile. Continuing, Winston said, "Actually, I'm a bit surprised that there doesn't seem to be much information about my earlier successes in all the books about me."

"You read books about yourself?" David asked innocently.

"Well, no, of course not," Churchill said, changing positions in his chair. "No, no. I've simply glanced through a few of them. I'm just saying," he went on a bit more forcefully, "that none seem to focus on anything more than my years during the war. As prime minister."

David nodded congenially, but he was really not well informed about Churchill's earlier life either. He hoped the man wasn't about to test him.

"I was merely mentioning the fact that in my own first act, I was secretary of state. I was colonial secretary. I was Parliament's chancellor of the exchequer. My point being . . . I did not lack for success. Then, during the '30s—and might I remind you that was an entire decade—I was out of office and out of favor.

"I was alone. By myself. Except, of course, for those who were close enough to point at me—usually as a good example of a *bad* one. Success, the ability to lead . . . all gone to the valley of the Shadow and all that." Churchill took a deep breath. "But!" He exhaled. "But I seemed to be the only one in that Valley at the time. And the view from there gave me a frightening perspective. While France and Poland and Belgium and our own prime minister fretted about taking lunches and talking appeasement and treaties, I alone in my hole could see what they could not.

"One cannot make peace with a monster. To attempt to do so is folly and merely baits the monster's trap. I saw Hitler rearming for war. And loudly though I rang the gong of warning, none would listen. Inevitably, when the Nazis invaded France and Poland and Belgium and our own prime minister resigned in shame, the British people came to the Valley . . . for they knew indeed where I resided. At that moment, my second act had begun."

David sat still, looking at the man who had lived it all, grateful for the unexpected view Churchill had provided him about how his own life had unfolded. Churchill sniffed and rubbed his face with a handkerchief. "Ah, well, I am excited about our quest. Happy to be a part, as it were."

David was about to ask if Churchill knew the question Gabriel would ask or if he knew where the others were. He was curious as to why Winston Churchill had been first to arrive and why he had been given time alone with the great man. But before he could utter a word, the door began to open.

CHAPTER 4

The two men shielded their eyes as the door opened fully. The light was almost unbearable, but Gabriel stepped quickly through and the door began to swing shut. As they stood, Winston muttered, "Here he comes. Don't call him an angel."

"What?" David responded, not certain that he had heard correctly and if he had, certain he didn't understand.

"This one's an *arch*angel," Winston quickly whispered as Gabriel approached, "and he doesn't appreciate being demoted by misidentification."

"Ah," David replied, not knowing what else to say.

"You'll see," Churchill said softly. Turning his attention to the new arrival, he boomed, "Good morning, Gabriel."

"Good day, Winston Churchill. Hello, David Ponder," Gabriel answered.

Without waiting for anything from their divine host, Winston stepped forward, did what came naturally to him, and went on offense. "When you say 'good *day*,' Gabriel, does that indicate morning, evening, or afternoon?"

Gabriel stood expressionless for a beat, then said, "I believe the human term is *grandstanding*, Winston Churchill. That is what you are doing, is it not? Grandstanding? Showboating?

Providing exhibition for our visitor? Surely you must remember we have had this conversation before." With that, Gabriel began to walk to the other end of the table.

David's eyes opened wide at what seemed like a rebuke, but Winston simply smirked and explained quietly, as if keeping a secret, "It's the same as the old 'inside or outside' question. I can't get a ruling on what time of day it is around here either. It drives me buggers. So to him"—Winston shot a thumb toward Gabriel and smiled—"I give a little of it back."

David suppressed a grin as they moved to follow the archangel. Turning when he'd reached the end of the table, Gabriel addressed the two when they had stopped in front of him. "This is the theater," he said, indicating with his eyes the room they were in. "Seating for attendees is provided in a circular environment. Guests are arriving now. Rules will be specified when all are seated. Take your places, gentlemen."

Before Gabriel had finished speaking, David noticed movement to his left. He cut his eyes toward the distraction, trying to remain attentive to the archangel, but found himself unable to stop staring at Daniel Boone. Or was that Davy Crockett? Suddenly, David broke into a sweat as people— some of whom he recognized, others he did not—poured into the theater. They came from the top just as Churchill had entered. David squinted into the darkness but could not see exactly where their point of entry was. Just as Winston's entrance had taken place, however, each person emerged from darkness to semidarkness, finally into full light, surprising David as each face was revealed.

But there were dozens of them. George Washington eased into a seat on the front row beside a woman who David thought might be Martha. He wasn't sure. Was Martha Washington a Traveler? How would *he* know?

There was a small Indian man in simple canvas clothes. David felt light-headed and put his hand on the table to steady himself. A man wearing a New York Yankees cap was shaking hands with Socrates or Aristotle or *someone* who was dressed in a toga. There were many attendees who did not seem at all familiar, and some whom David recognized but to whom he could not attach a name.

A few, however, were very obvious. They came down the stairs and spread into the seats. He recognized Eleanor Roosevelt. Some were talking quietly in twos or threes, others stared curiously at David, and several made eye contact. Louis Armstrong smiled, and so did Fred Rogers. David smiled back. Wow. He and Jenny had spent a great deal of time together in *Mister Rogers' Neighborhood* when she had been little.

There were people of all nationalities and manners of dress. Different time periods were apparent by their clothes and hairstyles. David saw several kings and queens, which prompted him to scan the growing crowd more closely. He was surprised that more royalty wasn't represented. Norman Vincent Peale seemed fascinated by something Martin Luther King Jr. was saying. He watched as King moved away and sat down on the second row beside a white-haired old man wearing jeans and a T-shirt.

David heard his name being called and turned to see Christopher Columbus waving wildly and pointing to himself, as if to say, *I'm here!* David grinned and waved back.

The gathering grew silent as David realized everyone's attention was on him. Upon that realization, he also became aware of a drop of sweat beginning to roll down from his hairline. "David Ponder?" he heard Gabriel say, and when he looked, the archangel gestured toward the other end of the table. Turning, David saw that Winston had already taken his seat. He hurried toward the British prime minister and quickly took the seat beside him. Both men were where they had been before.

"The head of the table," Churchill hissed out of the side of his mouth. "Sit at the head of the table."

David kept his eyes on Gabriel but shook his head no to Winston, who looked horrified. Gabriel lifted an eyebrow but said nothing. Leaning forward slightly and placing his fingertips on the table in front of him, the archangel began to speak. "Welcome, Travelers. Some of you, I have met. Many, I have not. But to all of you, I bid greeting. We are assembled here in order that humanity might have a final opportunity to right its ship, thus altering the direction people have chosen, many by default."

The archangel looked at David. "As you are aware, time itself is already racing by." He turned and reached behind him.

From an upright wooden case that David could have sworn was not even in the room a few minutes ago, Gabriel effortlessly lifted a large gold hourglass and walked toward the seated men to place it in the middle of the table.

"In the period allotted by this timepiece," Gabriel said to everyone present, "you must answer the following question correctly." He removed a small parchment from his robe and read, "What does humanity need to do, individually and collectively, to restore itself to the pathway toward successful civilization?"

David saw several within his sight line frown. He wasn't sure he understood either. "Excuse me," he said. "Gabriel, the question is about success? How to make ourselves successful? Like . . . economically? As people? I thought this would be deeper somehow. I'm not sure I get it."

If it were possible for a facial expression to be patient and impatient at the same time, this is precisely how Gabriel appeared. "I agree with your last statement, David Ponder. For quite some time, as a simple servant, I have trusted that He understood that fact about you—that you do not, as you so eloquently expressed, 'get it.' Perhaps you and Winston Churchill might devote some of the apportioned time to understanding the question before you begin the process of attempting to answer it."

David didn't have to wonder if *that* was a rebuke. He remained in eye contact with Gabriel and, in response, simply nodded. Taking a breath, placing the parchment on the table, and continuing in a gentler tone, the archangel said, "These are your precepts. First: You, David Ponder, as the leader of this assembly, may ask for as many as five advisers in addition to Winston Churchill—these can only be requested one at a time, as needed, by saying aloud, 'The summit requests the assistance of a Traveler.'"

"These five have already been chosen, though they are currently unaware of their possible participation and will remain so until the moment they are requested.

"Second: Though your time has a boundary, I would urge you to make use of a brief hiatus between each new adviser to your summit. During this break, the Travelers in attendance are free to discuss with one another what has been said and what they believe to be the answer to the question. It is assumed that in the time you allow them for discussion, they will influence the next adviser's contribution to your counsel.

"Third: During these breaks, neither you nor any member of your summit may have any conversation or contact whatsoever with the larger group, though you are certainly free to talk among yourselves. As always, there will be common language between Travelers. Language of origin is of no consequence. Each will understand the other.

"Fourth: Presuming the time will be used wisely, you will have five opportunities to answer the question correctly. You may only add Travelers as advisers to your summit one at a time. Each, if needed, is to be called immediately after any incorrect answer. Again, you have five opportunities to submit a solution. That solution, David Ponder, is to be presented by you or by the spokesperson of your choice. At that moment, I will inform you of success or failure.

"Fifth and finally: I am the arbiter. I have been given the authority to present and enforce these mandates. However, I will not remain in this place with you as you proceed. You, David Ponder, may summon me with the words, 'I am ready with the answer.'" Gabriel paused and looked carefully into David's eyes. "Is there any question about your guidelines?"

"No," David answered quietly.

Gabriel nodded. "Wisdom is the key, David Ponder. You have been chosen to lead this summit in an attempt to solve what, to mankind, has become a dire mystery." The archangel paused, as if deciding whether to say more, then added, "The entire answer is a mere two words. Part of me wishes I could go ahead and give you those words, but another part of me is disdainful, knowing that He has already provided you ample knowledge and opportunity to avoid this moment completely. After all, David Ponder, you no longer live in the time of law, but of grace.

"Though you do not know the men and women gathered here, they know you. And they trust that your own search for wisdom has prepared you for this task. Now lead them in the quest that will determine the future of their descendants."

Gabriel stepped away from the table. No one moved. Not a word was uttered until the archangel had almost reached the door. Then, breaking the silence like a clatter of spoons on the floor, Churchill rasped, "There's quite a bit of sand already in the bottom." Winston stood and leaned over to inspect the hourglass that had been placed in front of him. "The sands have been falling for some time. Aren't you going to reset it? Don't we get to start at the beginning?" He looked at Gabriel, who had stopped at the sound of his voice.

Gabriel said nothing at first, and David thought he might resume his exit and ignore the prime minister. Instead, he turned around and responded, "No one is *ever* allowed to go back to the beginning. However, the commencement of the second act is a matter of choice. For each person, the second act begins when and if one decides to change direction and set a new course. You of all people, Winston Churchill, should know that."

They stared at him, hushed by the truth in his words, but Winston, never shy and ever game to engage the archangel, spread his arms and asked, "Well then, exactly how much time do we have left?"

Before turning quickly and walking through the doorway, Gabriel processed what he had heard. Tilting his head slowly, his blue eyes like ice, he said, "Good question. Exactly how much time *do* you have left?"

━━●◆●━━

As the door closed, there was murmuring from those gathered, but as Winston sat back down, they grew quiet. "Suppose we get started," he said quietly to David.

"It sounds like we'd better," David replied. "Do *you* understand the question?"

"Actually, as you quite obviously also felt, the question seemed to me plain and straightforward," Winston admitted. "However, the winged one's impertinent response to your own query leads me to fear that the answer might be more complicated than I first assumed."

David nodded. "I agree. So before calling the first participant, let us study the question."

Reaching for the parchment Gabriel had left on the table beside the hourglass, Winston handed it to David. "Read it again," he said.

Glancing briefly at the assembly of Travelers, who were in rapt attention, David read in a loud voice so that all could hear, "What does humanity need to do, individually and collectively, to restore itself to the pathway toward successful civilization?" Looking to Winston, he added, "Thoughts?"

With an unlit cigar in his mouth, Churchill responded without hesitation. "You and I heard the word *success* and made an erroneous deduction most likely wrapped up in our human preoccupation with success as it refers to monetary gain. Glad you got it out of your mouth first." He grinned wryly. "Our arbiter doesn't seem to need additional prompting to demonstrate displeasure with me."

David agreed, but he didn't want to say so. Instead, he continued with a thought about the word Winston had singled out. "Most people have different things in mind when they are asked, 'What is success?' versus 'What is a successful life?'" Looking down at the parchment, he noted, "The question specifically refers to 'successful civilization.' That would signal to me that we should probably ignore the word *success* as it pertains to money or material possessions alone."

"Hmm . . . yes . . . *alone* being the key word in your assessment," Winston inserted. "Money must be a part of it, of course. Surely a 'successful civilization' must be economically prosperous."

David concurred and began rereading the parchment. "'What does humanity'—that's all of us, everyone—'What does humanity need to do, individually and collectively'? So, first, that tells us that there is something we *can* do. Second, it must be done alone—by ourselves—and as a group at the same time in order to be effective. Our answer must reflect that condition."

"Yes," Winston said. "Well noted. All right. Move on. The next words, 'to restore,' would lead us to believe that the answer will not be anything new or original. On the contrary, 'to restore itself to the pathway toward . . .' indicates that the pathway has now been abandoned."

David pursed his lips. "And to abandon a pathway, one would have had to be on it in the first place."

"Precisely," Churchill said with a sly expression. "The pieces, it would appear, are beginning to fall into place."

Not quite ready to believe they were finished with this, the first part of the enigma, David pushed on. "In addition, 'to restore itself to the pathway toward' would imply that it is the *direction* in which humanity is heading that is troubling. And that we were, at least at one time, headed in a more promising direction."

"The Principle of the Path," Churchill said without elaboration.

"The what?"

"The Principle of the Path," Winston repeated, chewing his cigar. "It states that direction, not intention, determines destination. Think about it. Certainly, humanity may 'intend' all it wishes. However, it is not what we *intend* to do or wherever we *intended* to be that results in a successful life, or in this case, a successful civilization. No! Rather, it is our pathway—*that specific direction in which we journey*—that ultimately determines our destination."

David continued. "And that destination for which we should strive is one of a successful life, not necessarily a life of success."

"Yes," Winston said, narrowing his eyes. "Therefore, in light of the question, it would seem that we are to work toward a successful civilization . . . not merely a civilization of success."

They sat quietly for a moment, each staring at the parchment, turning every word over and over again, aiming to be certain they understood the task they were about to undertake. Finally, it was Winston who spoke. "Interesting," he said and took a deep breath. Fixing David with his eyes, he said, "Well then, my friend. Let me ask you a question: What does humanity need to do, individually and collectively, to restore itself to the pathway toward successful civilization?"

David smiled. "That is the question, isn't it?"

"Yes," Winston said. "It is. And the answer, as we shall endeavor to remember, is a mere two words. Two words. Are you ready to begin?"

As David answered affirmatively, they both noticed smiles in the theater around them. Everyone seemed convinced that they'd effectively uncovered any hidden meaning and that the substance of the question was now completely in sight, ready to be answered. Confident that the hardest part of the quest had already been traversed, David readied himself to summon the first adviser, who, he felt certain, would be able to guide them to the answer.

———

"The summit requests the assistance of a Traveler."

With those words, David seemed to have set the theater in motion. After a second's hesitation, the attendees were turning or leaning to see who would approach the table. Several even stood up to look around, most focusing their gaze into the shadows, where it was harder to see. At first, David thought John Adams was the chosen Traveler, but quickly realized he was only crossing the floor to speak with Thomas Jefferson, who was seated on the other side.

David felt a hush come over the gathering that started at the end on his right and moved rapidly through the theater. As he and Winston stood, David was aware of John Adams passing behind him and returning to his seat. Trying to ignore the second U.S. president, who was for a moment within reach, he peered into the darkness where the attention of the Travelers at that end of the room indicated someone approaching.

At once, David saw the person moving briskly down the aisle. Head high and wearing a suit of heavy white cloth, the person's arms were adorned with brightly polished mail—small links of interlocking chain—from wrist to bicep. Leather boots and a scabbard carrying a huge sword completed the ensemble.

Before David noticed anything else, however, two things drew his attention. First, the white suit was emblazoned on its chest with a large red cross. Second, the person striding toward him was a girl.

"It's the Maid," Winston murmured.

David nodded, for he had recognized her too. The confident young person who had now stopped in front of them was Joan of Arc—the Maid of Orleans. "Bonjour, gentlemen," she said without smiling. "Where do you desire that I sit?"

"Bonjour, miss," David said and gestured to the table. "Wherever you wish."

Without hesitation, she rounded the head of the table and chose the seat in the middle, directly across from David. Before sitting down, Joan removed the scabbard from her belt with a practiced motion and placed it, sword and all, onto the table in front of her.

She was in her late teens. Her short, dark hair had been lightened by the sun, and its color made Joan's green eyes seem even paler than they were. She was a tall girl, David had observed when she approached, and now she sat ramrod straight in her chair. Not that it made any difference, but David also noticed an array of freckles scattered liberally across Joan's serious face.

David moved the hourglass to the side, having seen that it would obstruct the view between the three of them. Noting the sand's steady progress, he tried to put the time concern out of his mind for the moment and took his seat as Winston and Joan were getting settled.

Before he could say a word, Joan spoke first. "I am honored to be a part of this guild, Monsieur Ponder. I shall endeavor to be a productive component of the quest and leave my prejudices out of the process."

David's eyes widened. "Prejudices? I don't understand."

Answering, she said, "While commonality in language has been engendered between us in this place, dialect remains the same." Looking sharply at Winston, she added, "And I don't like his accent."

"Oh for the love of . . ." Churchill muttered, rolling his eyes dramatically and reaching into his suit pocket for a cigar.

"What do you mean?" David asked, confused.

"What she means," Winston said with feigned patience,

"is that my speaking voice, with its Old English intonation, gives her the creeps . . . the willies. Undoubtedly, the inflection with which I enunciate brings forth unpleasant memories." David's expression told Winston that his point still was not clear. Leaning closer, the prime minister loudly whispered, "Good God, man, think! My ancestors burned her at the stake in 1431."

Seeing recognition in David's eyes, Winston turned his attention back to his cigar. He had the Zippo out and was just about to spin the spark wheel when he caught sight of Joan glowering at him from across the table. He looked back at the lighter and froze. "Yes. Well," he said, clearing his throat and sliding the Zippo, along with the cigar, carefully back into his pocket. "My apologies, Maid." Then to David, "Onward, then."

"Joan," David began, "are you in agreement with our assessment of the question?"

"*Oui*, monsieur," the girl answered. Yes. "And I already know the answer."

CHAPTER 5

W hen Joan of Arc unexpectedly announced that she had already solved their dilemma, the two men across from her sat up straight. Winston sputtered as David put a hand out to quiet him, directing his full attention to the young girl. "You say you already know the answer?"

"*Oui.*"

David and Winston glanced at each other. David asked, "Are you positive? Did you talk with anyone else?"

"*Non,*" Joan said. No. "I did not speak with anyone else, but the answer is obvious. The answer is 'hope.'" She reached over, plucking the parchment from the table, and read, "What does humanity need to do, individually and collectively, to restore itself to the pathway toward successful civilization? The answer is 'hope.' Humanity has lost hope, and to restore itself to the pathway toward successful civilization, hope itself must be restored. Hope. Or, for two words . . . 'Restore hope.'" With that, she tossed the parchment back onto the table and added, "Call Gabriel now and give him the answer."

The three stared at one another momentarily before David, realizing he had been holding his breath, exhaled in a slow half whistle. "You don't lack for confidence, do you?" he commented, glancing at the hourglass. "We still have plenty of time. Let's not call Gabriel just yet. I suggest we test this possibility carefully before presenting a definitive answer."

Joan nodded. Hearing Winston chuckle, David turned and gave him a questioning look. Churchill held up his hands in mock surrender and smiled. "No, no," he said. "I'm with you. I also believe we must discuss the matter thoroughly. It's just that *my* answer, had you pressed me for one, would've been identical to that of the Maid's. Restore hope. I believe she is correct."

David shook his head and took a deep breath. "I'll admit, it sounds good to me as well. So let's talk. Joan? You first. How did you arrive at this conclusion?"

"Do you know my story, monsieur?" she asked in reply. Not receiving an immediate answer, she added, "Perhaps that might be the way to reveal the pathway to my answer."

"Perfect, actually," Winston said to David. He indicated Joan with his head and stated, "After all, hers is the only story of a human life that comes to us under oath."

"What do you mean?" David asked.

"The official records of her trial in 1431," Churchill explained, "and the Process of Rehabilitation—eyewitness testimony and documents proving her innocence—from several years later remain preserved in the National Archives of France. I've actually read them. The records are extensive and detail the facts of her life with remarkable fullness." Winston turned to Joan. "But I would consider it an honor to hear it all from you."

Their attention was rapt as the gathering in the theater

made not a sound. With a deep breath, Joan began. "I was born on 6 January, 1412, in Domremy, a tiny village in northern France. We were peasants. Not destitute, simply poor. My father and mother, Jacques and Isabel, were legally married. I mention this only because it was not always the case in those days. With my three older brothers and younger sister, I tended sheep and worked in the garden.

"This was during the time you now call the Hundred Years' War. For almost eight decades," Joan paused and, without a hint of warmth, looked straight at Winston, "the English vultures tore at our flesh."

Returning her eyes to David, she continued. "The French armies were in disarray. They were so demoralized by unrelenting defeats that the mere arrival of an English army was enough to cause a French retreat.

"It was the summer of 1424. The moment Gabriel first appeared to me, I was alone, drawing water from the stream."

"Wait," David interrupted. "Gabriel? I have read about you, too, Joan. In every account, it is written that you saw visions and heard voices."

Joan frowned slightly, an expression of impatience on her face. "Of course the scribes recorded visions, monsieur. How did you explain to *your* contemporaries that *you* had become a Traveler?"

Taken aback, David glanced at Winston and answered, "I didn't. I didn't tell anyone except my wife." Winston shook his head, indicating he had not told anyone at all.

"Did your wife believe you, monsieur?"

"No," David admitted. "Not for a long time."

Still glaring, but not quite so fiercely, Joan said, "Well, no one believed me either. I was twelve years old. Gabriel accompanied me on my travel and, during it, informed me that I would one day lift the siege of Orleans on behalf of the duke and bring the dauphin, Charles, to Reims for his coronation as king.

"When I returned from my travel, I told my parents what had happened. I told them about Gabriel and the military commanders I had met on my travel. I told them that I had talked to Saint Catherine and Saint Margaret." Joan paused and shook her head with irritation. "Of course, my family told our neighbors, and soon the whole village thought me mad. It was a childish mistake. I should not have uttered a word.

"Nevertheless, for the next several years, Gabriel talked with me. I went on another travel when I was fifteen. Then, in February 1429, the archangel announced that my time had come. I was only sixteen but managed to convince an escort of soldiers to accompany me on an eleven-day journey through enemy territory to the Royal Court at Chinon. There I presented my plan to the dauphin, Charles."

"What was your plan?" David asked.

"To sack the English, monsieur," Joan replied as if it were a stupid question.

Ignoring the tone in her voice, David asked another. "How did Charles respond to your plan?"

Joan shrugged. "He thought me mad as well. But he gave me troops. The dauphin knew that we French—his father and his father's father—had been under the English boot for three-quarters of a century. He really had no choice. Quite simply, I was his last"—Joan paused and lifted her chin—"hope."

David and Winston shared a glance. "What then?" David asked.

"We departed. I led the army to Orleans. We arrived on 29 of April. The siege on the city had lasted seven months. We took the English fortress in nine days."

David raised his eyebrows and looked at Winston, who nodded.

"We defeated the fortress built around the Church of Saint-Loup on 4 of May. On 6 of May, we took the fortress of the Augustinians, followed by Les Tourelles on the 7. The English lifted their siege and retreated the next day.

"These victories preceded our routing of the English at Jargeau on 12 June, Meung-sur-Loire on 15, and Beaugency on 17. The very next day, 18 of June, the English lost more than half their field army to us near Patay.

"After accepting the surrender of the city of Troyes, and every other town along the way, I led the men into Reims on 16 of July. Charles was declared *King* Charles VII. The following afternoon, I was at his side for the coronation."

Winston cleared his throat. "Might I ask, Maid . . . ," he began, and she signaled for him to continue. "At that time, during your extraordinary conquest of the English armies"—he paused to clear his throat again, trying to be tactful in what he was about to ask—"in the thick of the fighting, were you accompanied by our friend Gabriel?"

"No," she answered, and when she did, Winston and David nodded as if they had both been wondering the same thing. "No," she said again. "Michael."

"Pardon me?" David asked.

"Michael," she repeated. "Gabriel accompanied me on my travels. Gabriel informed me of my destiny. It was Gabriel who foretold the hope I would bring to a hopeless cause." Her green eyes narrowed. "But Michael attended me in battle."

"Oh dear," Winston said, his eyes wide.

"Michael, the other angel?" David asked Winston.

"Michael, the other *arch*angel," Winston corrected him, shaking his head, eyes wide in wonder. "Michael—patron saint of the warrior, field commander of the army of God. Oh dear. This does explain a lot. A sixteen-year-old girl crushing the military might of England and all that."

The two men turned their attention back to Joan, who was waiting patiently. "This is not new information," she said. "Look in your archives. Read the books. It's all there. I told everyone. I told them when I was twelve, and I told them at my trial. 'Gabriel and Michael,' I said. 'Gabriel and Michael.' No one would believe me."

"I am curious," David said carefully. Glancing around, he saw that the entire theater was riveted, anticipating the question they felt certain he would ask. "Where were Gabriel and Michael when you were—"

"When I was finally captured by the English? When King Charles refused to ransom me? Where were Gabriel and Michael when I was burned alive?" Joan finished.

"Yes," David said softly. "Where were they?"

Suddenly, Joan's face softened and she explained, haltingly at first. "Michael was terribly angry, monsieur. He had protected me for so long. Michael asked permission to kill them all but was ordered away. Gabriel . . . Gabriel was with me. He was with me at the stake. He knew . . . and I knew . . . that my destiny—my purpose—required that moment. And I have not a single regret."

Joan was silent for a moment then narrowed her eyes slightly and said, "Have you read of my death, monsieur? How it was carried out? The words I said as I took my final breath?"

David shook his head. He had not.

"Do so when you return to your time," she said. "Everything we do while we are alive—everything we say—is important. And though sometimes difficult, death is part of living. Sometimes, the *last* thing we do . . . the last thing we *say* . . . matters most. Often, it is all anyone remembers.

"My life was chosen to bring hope to my people. Hope is basic, like bread or water—one cannot live without it, at least not for long."

Winston spoke to David. "It's the first task of a leader, don't you know . . . to keep hope alive." Then to Joan, he said, "You have my utmost respect, Maid. Though it was my forebears you vanquished, your cause was just and true. Because of your actions, that thread of hope has continued unbroken for centuries. You are now the patron saint of soldiers; did you know? You are the patron saint of prisoners, of martyrs, of the Women's Army Corps—you are even the patron saint of the entire nation of France. Why? Because still, fair Maid, you inspire hope."

"Thank you, sir," Joan said. "From the beginning of my quest, I felt it to be my highest duty. Many said that my courage was responsible for our success, but it was hope. Hope is the captain of courage and the author of success. For the person whose hope remains unshaken has within them the power to do miracles. Hope sees what is invisible, feels what is intangible, and achieves what most consider impossible."

David said, "This must be the answer. When I lost all my worldly possessions, the one thing I never lost was hope." He thought for a moment then added, "It is only through hope that we persevere. Our lives may be swayed by gales of adversity . . . we may be drowning in the floodwaters of helplessness, but with strong hope, we continue the search to find a way when all evidence shouts, 'Quit.'"

"I have long believed," Winston said, "that there are no hopeless situations; there are only people who have grown helpless about them. When it came to pass that my tiny island nation was alone in the world . . ." Winston paused. He was no longer looking at Joan or David but staring at the table, as if lost in the memory.

"When the Nazis had consumed Europe, and America had yet to step forward, it was hope and hope alone that allowed me to rally my countrymen. It was hope that said, 'We shall fight on the beaches. We shall fight on the landing grounds. We shall fight in the fields and in the streets. We shall fight in the hills and we shall never surrender.'"

No one moved. Finally, Winston blinked and shook his head slightly. "I'm sorry," he said. "Seems like yesterday. My point was, I suppose, that as long as there is breath, there is hope."

"And that, monsieur," Joan said, smiling for the first time at Winston, "is the proof of hope."

"What, Joan," David asked. "What is the proof of hope?"

"That you breathe," she answered. "For if you are breathing, then you are still alive. And if you are still alive, that means you haven't accomplished what you were placed on earth to do. If you haven't accomplished what you were put on earth to accomplish, this signifies that your life's very purpose has yet to be fulfilled. If your very purpose has yet to be fulfilled, that is proof that the most important part of your life remains ahead of you!

"Don't you see? If the most important part of your life is in the future, then it doesn't matter how old you are or how sick you are. It doesn't matter how fearful or depressed you might feel or how penniless you might be. By the virtue of the fact that you still draw breath, there is more to come. There is more laughter and learning . . . more victories. There is more. This is the proof of hope, monsieur."

Winston laid his palms flat on the table and stood. To Joan he said, "We owe you a debt of gratitude, Maid. You bring us this answer—hope—that is shown to be the bountiful fruit of a very fruitful life. For your life was spent in the wickedest, most brutal time in history—the darkest of ages."

Churchill gestured toward Joan with an open palm and addressed the theater. "Ladies and gentlemen, I am beyond astonishment at the miracle of such a flower from such a soil." Looking to Joan again, he said, "Fair Maid, I am humbled by your presence, for I know that it was the sweat, sacrifice, and tears of your life that prepared the ground for a springtime of the human spirit."

To David and the audience, Winston finished in full voice. "Hope! Joan of Arc lived it, and now, I believe, she has provided the answer to our question. How will humanity restore itself to the pathway toward successful civilization? By restoring hope in one another! By restoring hope in the future! By restoring hope in humanity itself! Hope! Hope!"

The theater erupted in applause, standing, surprising Winston, David, and Joan, who were nonetheless happy that everyone agreed. "Restore hope" was indeed the answer!

When the ovation died away, David examined the hourglass. "There seems to be plenty of time left," he said. "Should we go ahead and call Gabriel?"

Joan smiled and nodded.

"Call him," Winston said.

Thinking for a beat in order to remember the words, with

profound relief and in a strong voice, David said, "I am ready with the answer."

Within a few seconds, the stone door opened, and with the brilliant light streaming around him and into the room, Gabriel stepped inside. Moving to the empty end of the table, the archangel spoke. "Hello, Joan of Arc. It is good to see you." She replied in kind.

Ignoring Winston altogether, Gabriel addressed David. "You have summoned me within a remarkably short period of time, David Ponder. I am eager to hear what you have to say. Proceed, please."

"Okay," David said, rising to his feet. "We do have what we believe to be the right answer." Joan was leaning forward, and David noticed that Winston had put a cigar into his mouth. It wasn't lit, but the prime minister had his arms crossed and was grinning smugly from ear to ear.

"Gabriel," David said, "we believe it is crucial that mankind not concern itself any longer with what we have tried and failed at. Rather, we should focus on what is *possible* for us to do. We are of the opinion that we should restore in one another the expectation of the *best* life has to offer—the spiritual, personal, and professional peace that we acknowledge has been offered to us.

"Knowing that he who loses money loses much, he who loses friend or family loses more, but he who loses hope loses all"—David paused—"our answer is that mankind must restore hope, Gabriel. Restore hope."

Gabriel had not taken his eyes from David since David had begun to speak, and he did not shift his gaze now. "You are quite right in your assessment of hope, David Ponder," the archangel said evenly. "The restoration of hope is certainly a necessary component in the solution you seek. But it is not *the* solution.

"Your answer—'restore hope'—is incorrect."

CHAPTER 6

D avid was stunned. As Gabriel strode from the room, he sat down weakly. Joan's head was bowed, and Winston's mouth was open, his unlit cigar in his lap. Everyone in the theater seemed to be talking at once. No one, it appeared, had foreseen this.

David looked again at the hourglass, then to his companions at the table. A few moments ago, they had been confident in the amount of time they had left. Of course that was because they were so certain of their course.

"I must apologize," Joan said to the men. "It was my rash behavior—my insistent nature—that has put us in this position."

"Nonsense," declared Churchill, tapping his fingers nervously on the table. "I was firmly in that corner as well."

"As was I," David said. "No cause for blame to be assumed by anyone. I'm sure I'd have come to that conclusion by myself."

Joan smiled gratefully. "The question is," she asked, "what do we do now? I was in my seat in the gallery when Gabriel posed the question. I was so certain of my answer that the mandates slipped by me."

"We have a few minutes to discuss this," David said,

"before requesting our next colleague." He indicated the others in the theater who were becoming louder and added, "Obviously, they are already in discussion. None of us—and by 'none of us' I am including them—has any clue as to which Traveler will be called with the next summons."

"I *hope*—" Winston said and then cringed. "Forgive me for even using that word at this particularly sensitive moment. Allow me to rephrase. As regards our compatriots who are now so deafeningly surrounding us, I *optimistically hold to the possibility* that their current conversations will bear fruit."

"So let's give them a few minutes more," David decided. "For now, with just us three . . . how did we so dramatically miss the mark?"

"Humph," Winston growled. "Never thee mind missing the mark. Where do we go from here?"

Joan closed her eyes. Speaking slowly, she recalled, "Gabriel did say that hope was a necessary component in the solution we seek."

"Hmm. Yes," Winston muttered, trying to concentrate despite the noise around them. All at once, they became distracted by the commotion of an argument between Albert Einstein and Thomas Edison. Many other Travelers had stopped to watch.

"Focus, my friends," Winston said drawing the attention back to their own conversation. "The Maid is correct. If 'hope' is a necessary component in the solution we seek . . ."

David finished the thought. "Then our answer was

not *totally* wrong. At least in some way, hope is part of the answer."

"Or will lead us *to* the answer," added Joan. "Of what great concept is hope a part?"

"Personality? Intellect?" David threw out.

"Leadership?" Winston asked.

For the next several minutes, they went back and forth, pitching as many possibilities as they could muster, but nothing they suggested gained any traction, and soon they were out of ideas. "At this point," David said, "I think we need to hold the concept of hope in the back of our minds. Let's remember that it is a confirmed piece of the puzzle that will fit into the answer, but I believe now is the time to go in a different direction. Are we ready to call our next associate?"

When Joan and Winston indicated their agreement, David stood up. At once, the gathering began to quiet. Benjamin Franklin waved his hand in between Edison and Einstein, pointing at the table to signal that the break was over. The two men, who seemed to be oblivious to everything except whatever it was they were so heatedly debating, hurried back to their seats. Franklin shook his head, shrugged, and smiled an apology to David.

When it was quiet at last, David glanced around but wasted no time. In a clear voice, he said, "The summit requests the assistance of a Traveler."

Just as before, heads swiveled and bodies changed positions, everyone eagerly awaiting the unveiling—for that is what it seemed to be—of the chosen Traveler. From row five in the curve, to the right of the head of the table, there was a small disturbance. Again, the lighting allowed David to see only half-bodies on that row as several people stood. He could, however, make out the figure of a tall man moving sideways down the row, excusing himself past those who were standing in an effort to reach the aisle.

As the man reached the end of the row, he took one step down. In the light, he looked up and smiled at David. David grinned broadly and moved away from the table. He was intending to greet the gentleman at the bottom of the stairs, but Winston grabbed his arm. "Introduce me," he said. "Don't forget to introduce me."

David tried not to laugh as he gently peeled Churchill's fingers from his bicep. "I will, Winston," he said. "He'll be sitting at the table with us." By this time, the tall man was down the steps, and within seconds, David had his right hand grasped firmly in his own.

"I was looking for you in the crowd, sir," David said. "I knew you'd be here. It's wonderful to see you."

"It's good to see you, too, David," the man responded. "You are just the person for this task."

"Thank you, sir. Right now, I'm extremely grateful you are here to help." David turned to the others. "Joan, Winston," he said. "May I introduce President Abraham Lincoln."

Both had stood as the president approached, and with the introduction, Joan bowed slightly as did Lincoln. Churchill, on the other hand, was a dervish of motion. He didn't seem to know exactly what to do. David was amused that Winston appeared to be awed by Lincoln. Winston Churchill, the man who saved the world for democracy in the twentieth century, was now demonstrating what he would later describe as "unbridled glee" at the opportunity to meet his own hero.

"Mr. President," Winston gushed as he shook hands with the much taller man. "I am honored beyond imagination to meet you, sir."

"The honor is mine, Mr. Churchill—" Lincoln got out before he was interrupted.

"Winston! Winston! Please *do* call me Winston."

"All right, then," the president said graciously, "Winston it is." Taking note of Joan moving to her seat, Lincoln asked, "Where would you have me sit, David?"

"Wherever you're most comfortable, sir," was the response. When Winston finally let go of his hand, Lincoln walked back around the table to sit beside Joan.

Adjusting his lanky frame in the chair, the president spoke first to Churchill, who was directly across from him. "David and I are old friends, of course. The young miss," he said, looking toward Joan, "seems like a friend to me because of the countless hours I spent reading about her adventures. But you, sir," he said diplomatically, his attention back on Winston, "have me at a disadvantage. While our time differential allowed you the opportunity to read whatever hogwash someone thought fit to print about me, I was not afforded the same pleasure."

Winston was about to say something, but Lincoln held up his hand and continued, "I am aware of your stature, of course. And after arriving here, I was offered the occasional chance to peek in on you, but having been through a war of my own, I just couldn't muster the enthusiasm to watch another. I must say, however, that your reputation, as I indicated, is quite well-known to me, and I consider myself privileged to be in your company."

Winston beamed. "Thank you, sir." Having a thought, he turned and said, "David, I know time is of the essence, but if you will allow me a very few seconds . . ." With permission assumed, Winston reached into the pocket where he kept the Zippo lighter and dug around for a moment with his forefinger. At last, successfully retrieving whatever it was he had been after, Winston grinned somewhat shyly and said, "Mr. President, I have carried this with me for years. But now, I would be honored to present it to you as a gift."

Lincoln looked intrigued. Whatever the object was, it must be small, for the prime minister had it grasped firmly in his fist, which was thrust onto the table. David and Joan leaned in for a better look as Winston opened his hand.

"This, sir," Winston said, "is a 1909 penny. A Lincoln penny, they call it in the United States. That was the first year it was produced. I acquired this particular coin through proper channels: my young nephew had it in his collection, and I took it." They all laughed.

"In any event, I have carried it with me ever since. It has

inspired me. Because you inspire me, sir. And now I want you to have it." With that, Winston reached across and placed the penny firmly into the president's hand.

David waited until Lincoln's appreciation had been expressed and the coin was in the president's pocket to bring the attention back to the mission at hand. "Mr. President," he began, "we could not see where you were seated earlier, but are we correct in assuming that you followed our discussion and the subsequent line of reasoning that led us to the first answer?"

"Yes," Lincoln replied. Looking at Joan, who was beside him, he said, "and might I add that I, too, was confident in the answer you put forth." He swallowed hard and looked back at David. "When Gabriel adjudicated your solution to be incorrect . . . frankly, I was surprised."

"During the break," David said, glancing briefly at the people surrounding them, "after Gabriel left, did you get any sense of what the others believe the answer might be?"

Winston and Joan studied Lincoln intently as he answered. "Well," he said with no hesitation, "the small group with whom I was deliberating seemed to agree on 'seek wisdom.' Some of them said it had been their first choice—it is, after all, one of the Seven Decisions. And that having been said, others of us—myself included—can certainly see how 'hope' would be a part of what should, in a successful civilization, be a lifelong search for wisdom."

Lincoln glanced past David and Winston, up into the

seats. Bringing his attention back to David, with a bit more volume in his voice, he said, "It occurs to me that perhaps—if there is another break—our friends in the audience might communicate more rapidly with each other than we did during the last respite in order to include an increased number of opinions. In that way, whomever is chosen to join us at the table might bring a firmer consensus than I have managed." The president grinned at his tablemates and continued even louder. "I know we are not supposed to communicate directly with the others, but it would be nice."

David heard chuckles around the theater. Smiling, he said to the others, "All right, then . . . wisdom. Seek wisdom. What do you think?"

"Certainly, we must explore the possibility," Winston said, and Joan agreed. Jerking a thumb toward the hourglass, he added, "But we might pick up the pace a bit."

David was tempted to tell the prime minister that picking up the pace might preclude giving coins to anyone else who arrived, but thought better of it. Instead, he asked, "Any suggestions about how we might test this proposal as a possible answer?"

"Let's define it first," Lincoln said. "Joan?"

"I am young," she replied. "I am not wise."

The president and the prime minister shared a knowing glance. Winston spoke first. "'In seeking wisdom, thou art wise; in imagining that thou hast attained it, thou art a fool.'" He sniffed. "Can't remember who said that, but I spoke the words most recently. Just now. You all heard me. Therefore, I'll take the credit."

They laughed as Lincoln took up the thought. "The wisest folks I've been around weren't at all impressed with their own wisdom. The wise seem always to be on a *search* for wisdom."

"Yes, well," Winston said, "and isn't that the world's terrible misfortune . . . imbeciles and extremists are always so sure of themselves. The wise seem to be full of doubts."

"Not doubts," Joan said. "Open . . . searching.

"Ah," Winston smiled. "So you admit to a bit of wisdom after all?"

Returning his smile, Joan responded. "I admit to nothing, sir." Then, cutting her eyes to the object that none of them could ignore, she said, "But I do believe that the more sand that has fallen from the hourglass of our lives, the clearer we should be able to see through it."

"Yes!" Winston said. "Young people know the rules. Old people know the exceptions."

"True," David said. "It's just that the older I get, the less likely I am to buy into the adage that age brings wisdom. Then again, I suppose one of the greatest pieces of wisdom one can attain is to become aware of how much you don't know."

"Which stimulates more passion for the search itself," Lincoln added. "I believe that it is the *search* that is the secret of a wise person. So at this moment, I suggest a search—not for wisdom, but *of wisdom*. As we appear to have hit on this as the probable answer, better we talk it out before offering it up." He looked around.

"Agreed," David said. "So define it first. That way we know what we're after. What is wisdom? Where is it? What are its aspects and features?"

The table was quiet for a bit, everyone turning over David's questions in their minds. Joan looked up. "Wisdom is found only in truth," she said. They all nodded.

After a moment, Lincoln lifted his hand slightly as if to ask permission to speak and stated, "I believe that wisdom is the ability to see, into the future, the consequences of one's choices in the present. The beginning of wisdom, however, is simply to desire it." Shrugging, he added, "Desire inspires the initial search, I suppose."

Joan again. "Patience is required before wisdom makes its presence known."

"Wisdom," Winston boomed, "begins in wonder."

"No person was ever wise by chance," David threw out. "I believe that. Don't you? And no one is born with wisdom."

"True," Lincoln said. "That's why wisdom in a young person"—he cut his eyes toward Joan—"is rare indeed." Shifting his weight in the chair and crossing one long leg over the other, he brightened. "How about this? Can we say that it is a characteristic of the wise that they don't do desperate things?"

"Yes. Yes," Winston exclaimed, patting the table. "Yes, wisdom is the attribute that prevents one from becoming entangled in situations where one needs wisdom! Ha!"

Chuckling, David asked, "So who is wise?" He looked at Joan. "I think we've already established the fact that wise people are humble. But *who* is wise?"

"The person who reads is a wise person," Churchill stated. "The person who manages to associate with wise people is wise—birds of a feather and all that. The person who questions opinions is wise." As an afterthought, he added, "Hmm . . . of course, the person who questions fact is a nitwit."

Lincoln narrowed his eyes as the hint of a smile showed in his whiskers. "Perhaps that is why our greatest scholars are not usually the wisest people." Noting the raised eyebrows around the table, he remarked, "Don't hold me in contempt for the comment. I'm only repeating what Geoffrey Chaucer said. And he is seated in row four—to my right." Lincoln grinned and cocked his head in that direction. "Geoff is the gent in the lavender suit."

After he had turned and looked with everyone else (and noted that Chaucer relished the attention), Winston expounded on what the president had said. "Folks confuse the two, you know—knowledge and wisdom. We can be knowledgeable with another person's knowledge, but we can't be wise with another person's wisdom. It is quite possible, after all, for *education* to sleep and snore in the filing cabinets of one's mind. But wisdom! Wisdom is wide-awake! And though shy and hiding it may be, once captured, wisdom is quite the reliable friend."

Changing the subject, Joan stated boldly, "I don't believe that age comes with wisdom."

"It *doesn't* necessarily," Lincoln replied. "Sometimes age just shows up all by itself."

"In what ways do we gain wisdom?" David asked, attempting to further the conversation.

"Reading. Association. I already mentioned those two," Winston declared.

"Through meditative moments by ourselves?" Lincoln offered.

"Yes, time alone," Joan affirmed. "Scheduling small patches of time for concentrated reflection."

"Imitation," David offered. "This may be the easiest way to gain wisdom, but it *is* what we do after reading about the lives of wise people or after associating with wise people. We imitate the behavior that we have observed."

"Good," Lincoln affirmed. "And true. I grew up in the backwoods of Kentucky. I didn't even go to school for formal education. Therefore, my writing, my manner of speech, how I learned to present myself . . . for the most part, has been a process of imitation."

"Experience," Winston said. "There's an old saying that goes, 'Experience is the best teacher.' That's not entirely true," he said. "I believe *other* people's experience is the best teacher.

Ha! Let them go through it, I say. I keep a careful eye out. If the water is warm, then *I* shall go swimming!" He thrust his head out comically toward Joan, making her laugh. "You see, dear girl," he said, "in the wisdom of the wise, there is an uncommon degree of *common* sense!"

"I feel that I gain a great deal of wisdom by simply remaining silent," Joan said.

With that comment, from the darkness came a loud laugh. Turning to see if he could spot the guilty party, Winston said, "Hmm, yes. It is the domain of scholarship to speak . . . the advantage of wisdom to listen. And I can only assume in good humor," he said to Joan, continuing in the same breath, "that your comment, while germane to the conversation and a noted building block upon which we will base our conclusion, was not directed at me."

Noting Joan's expression of innocence and desperately trying to hide his own grin, David steered the discussion in a different direction. "I have been mentally repeating our question," he said. "Everything seems to be on target. At least, nothing I have heard would lead me away from 'wisdom' as the answer. Let me pose this question: In what ways does wisdom become apparent in a life? How do people use it?

Lincoln thought for a minute then pointed to an old man in the theater. "That is Michelangelo," he said to David as the old man dipped his head in acknowledgment. "You may not have met him, but you are aware of his work. Michelangelo *carved* with wisdom."

The president gestured toward a beautiful black lady on the first row. "There is Mahalia Jackson. She *sang* with wisdom." And around the room Lincoln went, pointing out people and saying, "Charles Dickens wrote with wisdom. Helen Keller taught with wisdom. Rembrandt painted with it. Orville and Wilbur over there, they *imagined* with wisdom.

"I believe that wisdom, when harnessed over time, leads ordinary people in incredible directions. Long before their hands or voices produce greatness, wisdom shapes their minds and hearts.

"If we will only be patient and open, wisdom will reach out to us even from the Almighty's backyard. Mountains teach stability. The sun and the moon model faithfulness. The seas demonstrate our capacity to change. Even the tiny ant shows us about teamwork and dedication and thriftiness.

"Wisdom is the ability to discern. It is our perspective on life—our balance, our harmony. Wisdom is our understanding of how life works and our sense of humor when it doesn't. Wisdom is playful and caring. Wisdom ushers in good judgment, calms agitation . . ." Lincoln paused and made certain he had the eyes of everyone. "And if it is harnessed, wisdom just might restore humanity to the pathway toward successful civilization."

With a hush upon them, everyone knew that the moment had come to decide. Was this the answer they would present?

They had already failed once. David looked at the hourglass. "I don't know how much you watch the present time, but it surely seems that humanity is not behaving wisely right now," he said.

Winston poked out his bottom lip. "It is always a last resort," he said.

Lincoln smiled and nodded, but David asked, "What do you mean?"

Crossing his arms, Winston replied, "People and nations only behave wisely when they have exhausted all the other alternatives."

David tried not to appear surprised, but Winston's pronouncement seemed to him a particularly pessimistic view. Calmly, he turned to Lincoln and asked, "Mr. President, do you agree?"

Lincoln had his hands folded in his lap. His long legs were crossed and his head slightly bowed. Studying his hands, he answered slowly. "It is astonishing with how little wisdom mankind allows itself to be governed."

"That is because it requires wisdom to recognize wisdom," Winston said sharply. "The music means nothing if the audience is deaf."

Eyebrows were raised, but no one said anything. Then, still without having changed positions, Lincoln sighed and said, "Well, prime ministers and presidents may be the judges of the earth, but it is the people who judge prime ministers and presidents. Let us pray they are wise people."

"If they are not wise people," Joan said quietly, "or at least on the path to becoming so . . . then all is surely lost."

They were silent again, each in his or her own thoughts, yet furiously replaying what had been said, searching their minds for what might have been forgotten.

Finally, David said, "That's it, then? We are agreed?" Affirmed by all at the table, David glanced around the room and saw serious faces and nodding heads.

David took a deep breath, paused and held it, then said, "I am ready with the answer."

As before, the door opened immediately and Gabriel walked through. Without stopping, the archangel moved across the room, stopping only when he reached the open end of the table. Clasping his hands together in a relaxed pose, he said, "I am eager to hear the results of this particular discussion, David Ponder. I trust Abraham Lincoln was a welcome addition to your quest?"

"Yes, Gabriel," David answered. "He was. Thank you. Should I present the answer to you now?"

Gabriel gestured to the hourglass. "Whenever you wish," he said. "The time is yours."

Suddenly, David felt uneasy. Just a moment before, he had been so sure, so confident. Something about the hourglass— the sands of time steadily and unceasingly flowing, never to be recovered—made him weak. But this *must* be the answer, he told himself. By sheer force of will, David opened his dry mouth to speak.

"Gabriel," he said, "we believe that one of the reasons mankind has lost its way is our reliance on societal norms as life's blueprint. People have stopped questioning what the end result might be of certain actions and habits. We now rely on cultural trends—even celebrity behavior—to act as the compass guiding the decisions and behavior in our own lives.

"Therefore, we believe that to restore itself to the pathway toward successful civilization, humanity must individually and collectively begin to seek wisdom in our personal and professional lives—in ourselves and each other. Seek wisdom." David paused and repeated, "That is our answer. Seek wisdom."

"Yes, David Ponder," Gabriel said, and when those words were out of the archangel's mouth, David felt a sense of relief wash over him. The feeling, however, did not last long. "Yes, everything you said is true. Every assertion you made is accurate in its scope. Unfortunately, your answer to the question is incorrect. Yes, in order for the correct answer to produce miracles, seeking wisdom is an essential ingredient. But it is not the answer."

When Gabriel finished talking, he paused, met the gaze of everyone at the table, and walked out.

CHAPTER 7

I t had been so quiet when Gabriel left the room that David actually heard the stone door close. He felt cold and alone, though there were people all around. His elbows were on the table, hands clasped in front of him. When Lincoln reached across to briefly squeeze his forearm, David appreciated the gesture but still didn't know what to say.

That action by the president seemed a signal to the room that they could begin to move and speak. Meanwhile, all four at the table were dazed. The air had gone out of them; but quickly regaining their composure, they began to talk.

"Just as certainly as I believed hope was the answer," Joan said, "is how convinced I was about wisdom."

"Yes," Winston growled. "I felt that way as well." Reaching into his suit pocket and drawing out a cigar, he said to her. "May I smoke, my lady?" She nodded her assent. When the two other men declined his offer to join him, Winston stepped away to a place equidistant from the table and the first row of spectators. It was as close to "by himself" as he could manage, but he puffed away and the others left him alone. He was apparently, at least for the moment, in a foul mood.

David walked to the other side of the table, where Lincoln

and Joan were still seated. There, he got to one knee and said, "Do I look as scared as I feel right now?"

"Yes," Joan and Lincoln both said at once, causing them all to chuckle nervously. Winston couldn't hear what had been said but scowled as they laughed. He turned away, a great cloud of smoke like the aftermath of a forest fire rising about his head. It was impossible to distinguish the point from which Churchill's wispy white hair ended and the smoke began. It looked terribly funny to Joan, who suddenly began laughing out loud.

Soon, David and the president had joined in. "Winston will not appreciate our demeanor," Lincoln said.

"No," Joan agreed. "He will not." And for some reason that made them laugh even more.

Finally, wiping tears from his eyes with a handkerchief, Lincoln said, "I needed that. I think we all did. And the prime minister will be fine. We all have different ways of dealing with our stress. Some say there are times when laughing isn't proper. I believe otherwise. I believe that laughter—especially when shared with others—is an effective medicine for the head and heart.

"After Willie died . . ." He turned to Joan and explained, "Willie was my eleven-year-old son." He continued, "After Willie died, I read joke books for weeks. Some thought that insensitive. Mary certainly did, but I had to laugh—sometimes I cried *while* I laughed—but I had to laugh, or the grief would've done me in."

"So that's how Winston deals with stress?" David said as he motioned toward the man who was still by himself.

Lincoln nodded. "I suspect so. You watch. I predict he'll be fine in a moment. Soon he will be back to normal." Grinning widely, he added, "Which is only slightly less grouchy than that."

After sharing a last chuckle, the three got down to business. "I trust those in the gallery are taking your advice about talking to one another," Joan said to Lincoln.

"They are," he replied, scanning the crowd. "But what do *we* have? David, any ideas?"

"For some reason, I continue to explore the thought about what humanity lacks . . . or has lost."

"And what do you think that might be?" Joan pushed.

"If I had to answer right now," David said, "I think it is a boldness . . . Is that the right word? Something is missing in our leadership and in the way we conduct our own lives." He shook his head. "I'm all around it, but the thought is eluding me."

Winston came back at just that moment and motioned around the theater. "Move closer to the edge of the seats as I just did, and you can hear them talking," he said with a smirk. "Is that cheating?"

"If it was cheating," Lincoln replied with a smirk of his own, "Gabriel would have put us in a place where we couldn't have overheard. He only said not to discuss anything with the others. He never told us we couldn't listen."

They all smiled, and David caught Lincoln's eye. The president had been correct about Winston. The prime minister seemed back to his old self. "So what are they saying?" David asked.

All four were standing now, and Winston leaned in secretively. "Well, at first," he said, "everyone reacted to the archangel's rebuff as we did—in disbelief. There's a feeling that the question is a puzzle of sorts, which it most certainly is. 'Hope' and 'wisdom,' having been rejected as answers yet confirmed as a portion of what *comprises* the answer, have given rise to many theories."

"Such as?" Joan prompted.

"Mother Teresa and C. S. Lewis believe 'humility' is the answer. Not surprisingly, Douglas MacArthur and Marie Antoinette disagree." He looked at Lincoln. "Your great friend Frederick Douglass is effectively pressing for 'justice,' and there doesn't appear to be great opposition to his argument. Cleopatra and Dr. Schweitzer—along with that poet, Emily Dickinson—are gaining traction with 'love' or 'compassion,' but they don't seem to be defining their theme beyond the obvious."

"Any other possibilities?" Lincoln asked.

"Well," Winston said, "a few of the others are proclaiming 'faith' to be the only answer. Considering our present location, I considered it particularly bold of Mark Twain to loudly refer to their assertion as brownnosing."

Gradually, the four became aware of an uncommon silence

overtaking the room. As they looked about, except for a few scattered conversations still taking place, most in the theater were looking at a woman midway up into the seats on the side behind David's and Winston's chairs. Many people were nodding, and several near the woman looked at David and pointed at her. "Why are they pointing?" David asked the others. "Who is she?"

"That's the lady pilot," Winston said. "Earhart. Very nice. I talked to her last week. Amazing story. You wouldn't believe where she's been."

As David opened his mouth to ask where that might be, Joan interrupted. "I think they're pointing because she has the answer. Or at least an answer with which they agree."

"Don't ask," Lincoln cautioned. "That would break the rules." He glanced around. "Most everyone appears to be united with whatever she's advocating. And whether that is the case or not, I'm sure we can find out exactly what it is when you call the next Traveler."

"By the way," David said to Lincoln and Joan, "when I request a Traveler, how do you know to come to the table? How did *you* know that you had been chosen?"

"I heard the voice of the archangel," Lincoln said. "He wasn't in the room, of course, but his words were quite audible, at least to me."

Joan corroborated the president's statement by adding, "Yes, it was exactly like when I was a child—Gabriel was the voice in my head."

David shrugged his acceptance. Nothing seemed impossible or even odd to him anymore. "I think," he said, motioning toward the chairs as he moved to his own, "that it is time to try again." Arriving at a position behind his seat and having received no call for delay from the others, David said, "The summit requests the assistance of a Traveler."

This time, a man rose from the first row. He had been seated to the left of David and Winston at the end of the theater. David had noticed the man several times because he happened to be in his line of sight every time Gabriel stood at that end of the table.

The man was tall—not as tall as Lincoln, but taller than David. He had dark red hair that was parted on the side and combed neatly back over his head. He wore a gray suit with a white shirt and navy tie. He reached the table in no time and had spoken to Joan and was shaking hands with Lincoln when David and Winston reached him behind the chair at the head of the table.

The noise from the audience, which had been loud when the previous Travelers were summoned, was subdued. "Mr. Ponder, Prime Minister," the man said as he shook hands, "Eric Erickson. My friends call me Red or Eric . . . whichever you prefer."

"Nice to meet you, sir," David said. "Please have a seat."

As Erickson selected the other chair beside Joan, David and Winston returned to their seats on the other side of the table. David's mind was racing. Was he supposed to know who this was? When the man stood up, he had not sensed recognition flooding through the theater but assumed that surely he would know the man's name. Eric Erickson? Red Erickson? It was not remotely familiar.

David quickly looked again at the man. His clothes were not special in any way, but neither were they shabby. Except for a wedding ring, he was not wearing jewelry. His red hair was somewhat thin, slicked down with cream or oil, and combed in a style that made his receding hairline obvious. *Fifties*, David thought. *He looks like he is in his fifties. And he looks like he's from the '50s.*

Sitting down, David was not certain how to proceed. He glanced at the others. There was no hint of recognition in any of their faces. David reached for the parchment containing the question. He thought he might pretend to study it for a moment while he decided what to do. The room was holding its breath.

"That hourglass is not emptying itself any slower than it has been," the man said calmly to David. "There's not a lot of time to play games."

Somewhat startled, David looked up to see the man perfectly relaxed but with a gaze of steel focused directly and unwaveringly into his eyes. Shooting a glance at the others, David said, "I'm sorry? I'm not sure what you mean."

"None of you knows who I am," Erickson said bluntly but not in a rude manner. "Rather than wasting the time to figure out how to ask me, why don't you just ask me?"

David could feel himself flush. *How in the world does this man know exactly what is going through my head?* he wondered.

Erickson grinned. "Don't be embarrassed that I knew what you were thinking," he said. "It's just one of the odd skills I had to develop over the years."

David was flustered, but he managed to smile back at Erickson and say, "Okay, then, I apologize for being unfamiliar with you. Would you please fill us in?"

Eric leaned forward and placed his elbows on the table. "No need to apologize." Turning his attention to Churchill, he said, "Mr. Prime Minister? We never met face-to-face, and I'm certain you never saw a photograph of me, but in the limited correspondence we shared, you referred to me as 'Gallant Knight.'"

For a long moment, Churchill didn't say anything, and the others simply watched. Eric stared patiently at Winston with a grim smile, knowing the older man was seconds away from remembering. When he did, Churchill didn't know whether to laugh, cry, or have a stroke.

His faced paled and his jaw dropped. Inadvertently, his upper body moved forward as if to get a closer look at the person he thought he'd never meet. Winston's lower lip quivered as he blinked. "It can't be true."

They all looked back to Erickson, who chuckled slightly, raised his eyebrows, and lifted his hands a bit, smiling as if to say, *Here I am.*

"It can't be true," Winston said again. He stood and

proceeded to march around the table. "Sir," he said excitedly, "I intend to shake your hand." Erickson stood to receive the prime minister and did indeed have his hand shaken vigorously as Winston said again and again, "It can't be true; it can't be true!" and finally, "Gallant Knight indeed!"

David watched this spectacle with awe and consternation, having become more confused than ever. He had gotten to his feet again when Erickson rose to meet Churchill's advance upon him. Lincoln and Joan had also come up from their chairs, more to get out of Winston's way than anything else. Now they were all standing again.

Churchill had taken a couple of steps back from Erickson and was looking him over with pride and affection that reminded David of how a father might act after his ten-year-old hit his first home run. "My fine fellow!" he said. "I am simply in disbelief that we are able to meet—that I am able to meet *you*—at last. And under these circumstances!"

"Winston?" Lincoln said gently. "Perhaps we should be reintroduced."

"Yes! Yes!" Winston agreed, and with a flourish he gestured toward Erickson, who had been patiently enduring the prime minister's fawning with bemusement. "My dear friends, this is Eric Erickson, the 'Gallant Knight' to whom—come to think of it—I owe my own knighthood. Certainly, there is no doubt that I owe him the life of my beloved England." He turned to David. "Sir, I declare to you that we might owe him the life of America as well. Who knows what dastardly turn history might have taken were it not for this uncommon man." Winston suddenly took Erickson by the arm and thrust it into the air. "My friends, I give you Eric Erickson, the man who was single-handedly responsible for defeating the Nazi war machine in World War II."

David didn't know what to say or do, but as Erickson freed himself from Winston's grip, there was a small bit of enthusiastic applause up and to his right. Turning to determine its source, the group at the table saw two men standing and clapping. It was Dwight Eisenhower and the British general Bernard Montgomery—Monty—who had risen from their seats, bestowing a personal standing ovation upon their new arrival. While they looked on, Eisenhower, supreme commander of the Allied forces and later president of the United States, gave a thumbs-up to Erickson, who grinned sheepishly and waved back.

When everyone had returned to their seats, Eric glanced toward the two generals, commenting to Churchill, "I never met them either." Winston laughed as if it was the wittiest line he'd ever heard.

"Someone," David declared, "simply must tell us the story here. Fill in the blanks for me." Joan and Lincoln expressed their interest, and when Erickson appeared hesitant to talk about himself, Winston gladly took the floor.

"Let me begin," the prime minister said, "by bringing to light a fact that seems to have been swept under history's rug. The public at large, to this very day, has been blissfully unaware of the hair's breadth by which the Allies won World War II. We were so close to losing—being completely overrun by the Nazis—that it shakes me to the core . . . even at this moment."

David glanced up at Eisenhower and Montgomery, who were solemnly nodding their heads in agreement, and blurted out, "We almost lost? How have I never heard about this?"

Lincoln smiled and looked to Churchill. He knew the answer, and Winston confirmed it before continuing. "How did you not know?" he asked. "Because that fact is not discussed in your history books, my boy. And as you well know, history is written by the winners.

"Sit still and listen," Winston continued. He took a deep breath and leaned to examine the hourglass closely. Churchill seemed confused for a moment and tapped the glass with his fingernail. Frowning, he forced his attention away from the timepiece and gestured toward Erickson. "Because of our time constraint, I will relate this account as plainly as I can. Facts only; I will not exaggerate what I know. Neither will I speculate about what I don't.

"This man before you, Eric Erickson, is a product of Brooklyn, New York. Born into an impoverished family, he nonetheless rose through the ranks of education and hard work, subsequently earning an engineering degree from Cornell.

"Eric worked in the Texas oil fields for a number of years, then for Standard Oil and several other oil firms in Europe and the Far East during the 1920s. A gregarious sort, he made friends everywhere he went. He married a marvelous young woman—you'll see why I consider her marvelous momentarily . . ." Winston stopped his story and turned to address Erickson. "Sir, obviously I was not privy to a designation other than 'Ravishing Damsel.' Might I, at this late date, know her name?"

"Ingrid," Eric said. "And she is sitting right over there." He indicated a woman in the seat beside the empty one from which he had come. As everyone turned to look, Ingrid gave a tiny, self-conscious wave.

"Ingrid!" Winston repeated and bowed as formally as he could manage from his seated position. "It is my great honor, dear lady." Returning his attention to Eric, he said, "You will please note that our gratitude exists in equal measure for your lovely wife."

Looking back to the others, Winston continued. "In 1936, an extremely odd series of events was put into motion by Eric, slowly at first, but with increasing frequency during the next three years. By this time an extremely successful businessman—and one of no small fame—Eric set about trashing the reputation he had so carefully crafted his entire life.

"As Adolf Hitler was becoming known and despised the world over, Eric began to *publicly* express admiration for the man! He increasingly proclaimed Hitler's genius to anyone who would listen and pointed proudly to the Führer's significant contributions to correct thinking and a progressive world. And Eric became openly anti-Semitic.

"Soon, as you can imagine, friends and business associates began to avoid the Ericksons. This was especially so in 1938 after Eric loudly berated a well-known Jewish businessman in a crowded restaurant. This public dressing-down was done by Eric using particularly vulgar labels, offensive not just to Jews but to anyone with a conscience. The tirade was immortalized with a large newspaper article condemning Eric and anyone who associated with him. This, of course, included his dear wife, Ingrid.

"As for other family members—parents, brothers, sisters, Ingrid's relatives as well—Eric was disowned. Finally, with every friend he ever had bidding him good riddance, Eric Erickson did the unforgivable. He formally renounced his American citizenship. He and Ingrid moved to Sweden."

With those words, even knowing there was more to the story, David and Lincoln frowned, avoiding eye contact with Erickson. Winston continued. "Eric set up his oil exporting business in Sweden but didn't slacken the fervor or regularity of his public opinions that had already caused him to be ostracized in America. Soon he was just as well-known in Sweden for his pro-Nazi stance. And he was shunned there too. The only difference being that in Sweden, an officially neutral country, there were some who weren't afraid to openly agree with Eric.

Winston placed his cigar, which had already gone out, into the corner of his mouth and said to Eric, "Everything accurate so far?" When the red-haired man indicated that it was, the prime minister continued. "So, with his reputation spreading, it wasn't long before the men of the SD—this, the security division of the Gestapo who were stationed at the Stockholm embassy—contacted Eric. 'Germany,' they told him, 'has an acute need for oil. You, one of the world's leading experts on oil, might greatly help the cause of the Fatherland.'

"So a cautious proposal was made. 'Would Herr Erickson be interested in furthering the interests of the Nazi regime? Financial benefits beyond the norm would also accrue . . .' Eric responded with wholehearted eagerness.

"Erickson quickly provided the deals the Nazis were seeking and began to explore with them an expansion of their synthetic oil industry. Germany, at the time, was the world leader in the complicated technology required to produce synthetic oil. This was a process that converted coal into oil and obviously removed Nazi dependence on imported oil.

"No one—not the Americans nor the British—could obtain reliable information about the location of German refineries. The security, as you can well imagine, was rigorous. And ridiculously effective. In addition, the synthetic oil production plants were so well hidden, they might as well have been built underground. In fact—ha!—jumping ahead a bit, that's exactly where they were. Underground! Every blasted one of them!

"These synthetic oil plants were highly evolved, to the point that the Nazi war machine was indeed beginning to fill *all* its needs from the output of these hidden locations.

"Now," Churchill said, clearing his throat and grinning devilishly, "this is where the tale gets interesting. In late 1942, 'Gallant Knight' managed a meeting with Heinrich Himmler himself. Himmler—the very head of the Gestapo—a calculating mass murderer unequaled in the annals of history!

"There, in the psychopath's own office, Eric proposed to build a huge synthetic oil plant in neutral Sweden. Such a factory, he explained, would be safe from the possibility of Allied bombers, and running at peak capacity—in the event the German plants were damaged or destroyed—it would provide all the oil Germany would ever need.

"Eric provided export plans already approved by Swedish businessmen and bank financing arrangements already signed by Swedish banks. All he needed, Eric said, was the approval of Himmler, who would have to receive approval from Hitler himself. 'Might this also be a way,' Eric asked, 'in which personal funds could also be invested? Personal investment from Himmler,' Eric suggested, 'would not only speed the project along, but it would provide income for the Gestapo chief cached in Swiss accounts if, God forbid, things should go badly for the war effort.

"It was a brilliant proposal, of course. Genius, actually. Himmler fully embraced the idea, invested in it personally, and with Hitler's approval, ordered the project to begin immediately. Of course, for Eric to build a synthetic oil plant and to build one quickly"—Winston spread his hands and opened his eyes widely with an expression of innocence—"it was obviously *crucial* that Eric become familiar with the German technology he was supposed to reproduce in Sweden.

"Ha!" Winston slammed his palm onto the table. "So he went back into the viper's den. In Himmler's office again, Eric secured a top-level.Gestapo pass signed by Himmler himself. The pass waived all security clearances and requirements and authorized Eric to travel anywhere in the Reich, to investigate any oil refinery or synthetic plant he wanted to see. The pass further stated that he was to receive any information he requested from any plant expert or security personnel. Eric also secured an order, *personally signed by Adolf Hitler*, providing automobiles, drivers, and unlimited petrol coupons.

"In the weeks and months to follow, our friend here toured almost every oil refinery and synthetic plant in Germany and the occupied territories. He obtained detailed plans of the operations. He procured maps to and from the factories."

Winston glanced at the hourglass and paused. Once again, he appeared slightly confused by whatever he had noticed, but without telling the others exactly what that might be, he said, "Time is growing shorter, my friends. I could talk all day about this. I could write a whole book about it, and someone certainly should have.

"Suffice it to say, that by 1943, the German plants— underground locations included—began to be struck by persistent American bombing attacks." Winston's eyes twinkled as he warmed to his story again. "And these bombers were not only precise in their target acquisition, but mysteriously on schedule with return raids when a damaged plant was repaired.

"Within months, supplies of petrol from the refineries were drying up; and by the end of 1944, the synthetic oil production of the Reich collapsed in total. And so, while Luftwaffe planes still outnumbered our own . . . while their Panzer and Tiger and Panther tanks still outnumbered our own, they simply ran out of fuel to operate them. Little known, but true, the Messerschmitt 262—the world's first operational jet fighter— had already rolled off the assembly line. And in numbers! But they sat on the ground for lack of fuel.

"At the Battle of the Bulge, German soldiers created forts around their tanks when the petrol ran out. Lack of fuel forced three hundred thousand German troops to surrender in the Ruhr Valley. All across the European Theater, the war itself finally ground to a halt . . . for the enemy could no longer move.

"And it was all due to the efforts of one Eric Erickson, the Gallant Knight who now sits before you."

In the pause that followed, Eric shifted self-consciously in his chair. David didn't know what to say. He was astonished. First, at the bravery and selflessness this man had displayed in service to his country . . . to his world. And second, because he had never heard even a part of Erickson's story. Lacking any other words, David blurted out, "Is this true?"

"Every word of it!" someone yelled from the crowd in the theater. As heads turned, David realized that the affirmation had come from Eisenhower.

Seeing that the former supreme commander of the Allied forces had just attested to his narrative, Winston added, "General Eisenhower—excuse me, President Eisenhower— stated for the record that 'Eric Erickson shortened the war by at least two years.' Albert Speer, Hitler's minister of armaments and war production, testified at Nuremberg that 'the oil attacks brought about the end of the war.'"

Lincoln, who had been quiet, asked Eric, "Were you ever in danger of being exposed?"

"Constantly," Eric replied. "I recruited confederates in the occupied territories, and being back and forth to Sweden as I was, I never knew if one of my own spies had been caught and tortured by the Gestapo while I was gone. So returning to Germany was always tense.

"One of my people, Marianne von Mollendorf, was executed in front of me. She and I were looking into each other's eyes when she was shot. She could have turned me in, of course, but she didn't. And I could have spoken up at that moment . . ."

Winston saw the guilt and confusion in Eric's eyes and leaped into the void. "They'd have only killed you both, my boy. You know that. There was no other choice you could have made. You stopped the war."

"I suppose," Eric said flatly. "That's what everyone seems to think."

Winston pushed on. "Eric? Eric, listen to me. May I tell you something of which you were never made aware?"

"Sure," Eric responded.

Winston looked to Eisenhower, then back to Eric. "Actually, I signed papers—as did several others—swearing that what I am about to tell you would never be divulged." Lincoln, Joan, David, and everyone else in the room were at full attention. "I've thought about this many times, and frankly, since arriving here, I've had no one I wished to tell. Being in this place, however, renders my promissory signature rather moot, wouldn't you think?"

Eric smiled.

"In any case," Winston said, "here it is. Your exploits, though most have been unknown to humanity to this day, saved hundreds of thousands of lives. But I will now reveal to you that it was much bigger than that. Well after the war, upon examination of German records and top-secret testimony connected with those records, we discovered just how vital your work truly was.

"All the refineries and synthetic oil plants were targeted, of course. But the bombing of one particular location—the synthetic plant at Merseburg-Leuna—just happened to destroy a building in which experiments were being conducted with heavy water. For Germany's atomic bomb project." He paused and leaned forward. "Word was, my boy, that without your information—without the destruction of that particular building at that particular time—Hitler would have wielded the bomb well before the end of the war."

After the appropriate hard swallows that information

caused, David said, "You're absolutely right, Winston. We owe a debt to this man. Eric," he turned and asked, "did your family and friends find out the truth about you after the war?"

Managing a smile, Eric said, "Yes. And that was a great day for Ingrid and me. Except for one other friend of ours, Ingrid bore the whole burden of this matter alone.

"Several months after the war was over, the State Department held a special dinner. It was all a big secret. Our families, former friends, businesspeople—a huge crowd was invited, and they didn't know why. When they were all seated, an American embassy official got everyone's attention and announced the guests of honor. Ingrid and I had been hidden offstage, and when we walked out, the audience literally gasped. Quickly—before they could stone us, I thought—American officials told the whole story. Or at least as much as they could. It was a tearful reunion with our families and friends . . . and I suppose all's well that ends well." Eric shrugged. "And that's it, I guess."

"Winston is right," David said. "We really *could* talk about this for hours, but we have to move on. Thank you again for all you did."

Eric nodded.

"Okay to continue with our next answer?" David asked. "Can you guide us into this discussion?"

"Sure," Eric replied. "Let me start by telling you what the majority of the Travelers think the answer is." Around the table, they listened attentively. "Before I lay this one out there, I've got to say that I feel a bit odd having just had my life's story revealed and now having to tell you this answer. Or what we think is the answer."

"Why? What is it?" David asked.

"Be courageous," Eric said, "or 'show courage,' or any other two-word way you want to put it. Why two words, anyway? Never mind," Eric added quickly, answering his own question. "We haven't got time to figure that out too. In any case, 'have courage' or 'be courageous.' Courage is our answer. I didn't come up with it, but I think I agree."

"No time for modesty, Eric," Lincoln said. "Maybe that's the reason you were chosen to join us. It certainly took a great deal of courage to do what you did. So let's explore this quickly." He gestured toward the hourglass. "If we need the last two opportunities after this one—and I pray that we don't—we need to conserve some time."

Eric said, "Everyone who hears my story seems to assume that somehow I was never afraid." He rolled his eyes. "I was always afraid. I just managed to do what I knew I had to do . . . anyway. So to make sure we don't get off on *that* foot, courage is resistance to fear or mastery of it, but it is not the absence of fear."

"I agree," Joan said. "Perfectly expressed."

"There is an odd paradox attached as well, though," Eric shrugged. "That boldness . . . that assured air—it is strange to me that sometimes a person has to be a little careless with his life in order to keep it."

"What is courage?" David asked. "Define it. Start there."

"It is a virtue," Winston said. "It is a mystical virtue before which difficulties shrink and obstacles crumble into dust."

"Courage is not merely one of the virtues," Lincoln observed, "but the form of every virtue at its testing point."

"Well said," Winston replied. "But Mr. President, you must at least concede that courage is the greatest of the virtues. After all, if one hasn't courage, there might not be opportunity to display any of the others."

Lincoln chuckled. "You are correct, Mr. Prime Minister," he said agreeably. "Without courage, even wisdom would bear no fruit."

"Is courage a form of power?" David threw out.

"*Non*," Joan asserted. No. "I believe everyone possesses the *power* to achieve whatever they wish. Many, however, lack the courage to do so."

Eric spoke. "Courage expands the minds and hearts of others in its presence. It is contagious. One person with courage forms an immediate majority, and others are caught up in his wake. When a brave person takes a stand, the spines of others are stiffened.

"But here is something curious," Eric continued. "The opposite of courage is cowardice, I suppose. In any event, I believe that courage enlarges our possibilities. But cowardice diminishes the odds of everyone's success in any endeavor. I have personally experienced physical danger because of the cowardice of others. Because we as people and nations are so connected, the fears of the fainthearted increase the hazards that jeopardize the lives and the freedoms of the brave."

"How does one become brave?" David asked.

Eric raised a hand. "I don't mean to talk too much," he said, "but I can answer that if you wish."

"Certainly," they all said at once and leaned forward to hear how he intended to reply.

"I believe strongly," Eric said with conviction, "that whether you are a man or woman, boy or girl, you will never accomplish anything without courage. It is the greatest quality of the heart except honor. That having been said, I believe that every man, woman, boy, and girl already possesses deep within an abundant supply of courage. But that courage only appears—seemingly spontaneously—when we care very deeply about something or someone. It is at that moment when we take risks that are unimaginable in any other context."

"Bravo," Winston said and clapped several times as the others acknowledged the truth of the words Eric had spoken. "Many a victory was turned into a defeat for want of a little courage."

"Is 'show courage' the answer, then?" Joan asked. "If everyone possesses courage, is the utilization of the virtue, to actually 'show courage,' what humanity needs to do in order to restore itself?"

"I am of your time," Eric said to David, "and I think courage is the answer." Indicating Winston, Lincoln, and Joan, he said, "It may be cynical to say so, but with rare exceptions, people aren't electing leaders like this today. A nation that has *forgotten* the quality of leadership it took to make a civilization great in the past is not likely to insist on greatness in its leaders today."

"I believe we *have* forgotten the display of courage it took to mold what humanity once was," David said. "This makes me more and more confident that courage is what we need, individually and collectively." To Churchill and Lincoln, he asked, "What was the historical perspective in your time? And in yours, Joan?"

Joan spoke first. "I always found it strange that physical courage was so common and moral courage so rare."

"I'm not sure that has changed," Eric said and added, "Sorry. There's my cynical side again."

"I dealt with folks as divided over issues as any group since time began," Lincoln said, casting his eyes upward as if searching his memory. "When there are those who disagree with us, it takes courage, certainly, to stand up and speak. But it also takes courage to sit down and listen. Courage can be the bridge to wisdom. Life, despite its heartbreak and agony, cannot be unlived. But if our mornings are faced with courage and wisdom, the past need not be lived again."

"Hope and wisdom?" Joan asked. "Are they a part of courage?"

"Yes," Winston answered definitively. "But is courage the answer?"

"We want to *restore* civilization to the pathway," Eric said.

"Do you think there is less a display of courage now than there used to be?"

"Maybe there are not as many opportunities to be courageous?" David proposed.

"Oh, that is ridiculous," Winston scoffed. "Those who lack anything—courage, wisdom, and hope included—will always find a philosophy to justify it. What rubbish! And of course, as part of their justification, they cast suspicion on anyone who has proper motives. People with courage and character always seem sinister to the rest!"

They laughed. Certainly, no one could dispute those words. When they settled again, David asked, "Are we ready?" No one wanted to answer, so for a beat, they just looked at him, then laughed again. It was nervous laughter, to be sure, but finally, David said aloud what they all had been thinking. "Wow. I am about to call Gabriel again."

David looked at the hourglass. "I *hope* that our *wisdom* has led us to *courage*." They all smiled, but Eric said, "When we are through with all this, David, remind me to tell you how bad that joke really was."

David smiled grimly and said, "I hope we are laughing when all this is through." Then, in a loud voice, he said, "I am ready with the answer."

CHAPTER 8

As Gabriel entered the room, he walked straight to the end of the table, taking the same position he had before. The archangel made a point of examining the hourglass before clasping his hands in front of himself. "David Ponder?" he said. "Have you arrived at a conclusion?"

David stood. "We believe so, Gabriel."

"I am eager to hear your answer."

David glanced at the others around the table and began. "Taking into account your words about 'hope' and 'wisdom' being a part of the answer, we have arrived at what we believe is the logical choice." David paused and decided to avoid any preamble this time. *There is no explanation needed*, he thought. *This has got to be right.* "Gabriel," he said, "The answer is 'Show courage.'"

Gabriel did not respond immediately. Nervous to begin with and now even more so, David found it impossible to match the archangel's silence and began to talk despite having decided not to. "Hope and wisdom are necessary components to effective courage and to restore civilization to the proper pathway . . . Well, it sure seems that people used to be more courageous . . . Morally courageous, we believe . . . Obviously, there are—"

"The answer is incorrect," Gabriel interrupted, and without delay he stepped away from the table and started for the door.

Winston balled up his fists, muttered to himself, and reached for his cigar. David didn't move from where he had been standing but was aware of the blood draining from his face. He looked at Lincoln, who appeared sympathetic and encouraging at the same time. Joan's brow was furrowed in confusion, and Eric simply sat still with his eyes closed.

The massive door was opening, and those in the audience were beginning to rise to their feet, talking softly to each other—yet all eyes were on the departing archangel. He was almost to the open doorway, its intense light radiating through the room as it reflected around his flowing robe and wings. Suddenly, to his shock, David heard his own voice rise above the increasing noise of the theater. "Gabriel!" he called out.

At once the room grew quiet. The archangel stopped in midstride. Cocking his head as if not believing what he had just heard, Gabriel slowly turned, but only halfway around. "Yes, David Ponder?" he asked.

David could hear his own heart beating, the blood rushing through his ears. He felt his mouth open and heard himself gasp like a schoolboy caught misbehaving by the principal. The archangel's face was not threatening, but neither was his expression patient or kind. Gabriel raised an eyebrow. "Yes, David Ponder?" he repeated with a bit more volume.

David did not know why he had shouted at that moment.

Frustration? Confusion? Fear? In any event, not knowing why he had stopped the archangel's departure, he was now without a clue as to what he wanted to say. "Ah . . . Gabriel?" he managed and paused again, but this time, the archangel did not answer. Mentally scrambling and uncomfortably aware of the stares from everyone in the theater, David plunged ahead and said the only thing that came to his mind. "May we ask you some questions?"

Without hesitation, Gabriel answered, "Certainly," and moved to return to his place at the table. As the door closed behind the archangel, David looked at the others in amazement. They returned his expression with disbelief of their own. In fact, the entire audience seemed flabbergasted at this turn of events and Gabriel's casual acceptance of David's panicky request.

As always, Gabriel stood while David sat down with the others. This move, on David's part, was executed more because of weak knees than any etiquette he might have thought to observe. "I didn't know we could ask questions, Gabriel," David said, still somewhat shaky. "Actually, you didn't mention that we were allowed to ask you anything."

Gabriel replied, "That is correct. Neither did I say that you could *not* ask questions."

"Sir?"

"Yes, Eric Erickson?"

"Sir, is there anything *else* that we might have overlooked—of this sort, or any other sort—of which we are unaware at this time, that is available as a resource to us in our quest?"

"Very good *first* question, Eric Erickson," Gabriel replied, "but no, I am your only resource."

"Ha!" Winston cackled. "Very good first question indeed. Just the kind of query I would expect from a spy! Now. Down to it. What shall we ask the *angel*?"

"Archangel," Gabriel corrected immediately.

"Oh yes. My apologies," Winston responded as he winked at David.

"I have a question, sir," Lincoln said. Gabriel turned his attention to the president, who asked, "You revealed to us earlier that 'restoring hope' and 'seeking wisdom' were parts—we assumed integral parts—of the correct answer. Is that also true of 'showing courage'?"

"Yes," Gabriel answered. "Courage is necessary for wisdom and hope to fulfill their roles as effective virtues. Likewise, wisdom and hope—as you correctly ascertained—must be present for courage to achieve its highest value. Yes. All three—hope, wisdom, and courage—are components of the answer you seek."

"This answer," Joan said carefully, "when we find it . . . will it change the world?"

"It is the only thing that ever has," Gabriel said.

"Are we expanding our thinking past the point we need to search?" Winston asked. "Are we making this too complicated?"

"Yes and no," Gabriel replied.

"Ah!" the prime minister said as sarcastically as he could manage. "Yes, then. Well, thank you so much for the map you've provided with *that* answer. We'll take it from here and go directly to the treasure."

"I understand your question, Winston Churchill," the archangel said, "and I will ignore your childish comment. While the answer you seek is simple, I despair of your ability to find it easily. Yes, your thought processes are rational, but as humans you are much too egotistical to succeed in this search quickly. Or at all."

"Please, Gabriel," Lincoln said, shooting a warning glance to Winston, "be patient with us a bit longer. We are trying to understand. What do you mean by 'egotistical'? I don't wish to disagree with you, but I feel that presently we are as humbled by this process as we could possibly be. I, for one, don't feel smart or capable right now . . . or egotistical. So again, please help us comprehend what we are up against."

"What you are up against, Abraham Lincoln," Gabriel began, "is your very nature. When I used the term *egotistical*, I didn't necessarily mean you at this table—with one possible exception." Pausing, Gabriel turned to stare directly at Winston, who smiled as if he had been given an award. Continuing, the archangel said, "It is humanity's egotistical nature to which I was referring."

"I'm still not sure I understand," Lincoln said. "Please . . . if you will . . ."

"As human beings," Gabriel said, "you seem to assume that you are the possessor of mankind's greatest moment. You believe that everything existing on earth at this time is the pinnacle of achievement. Humanity is proud."

"Pride goeth before a fall," Joan murmured to the others, who nodded without taking their eyes off Gabriel.

"As humans," the archangel said without missing a beat, "you think you are stronger than ever before. You worship your own intelligence. You've been to the moon and consider *that* a grand accomplishment, yet you are not clever enough to find the clues He left you about who made the moon in the first place!"

Winston opened his mouth to speak. "I am not finished, Winston Churchill," Gabriel said sharply, his eyes flashing. Pressing on, he said, "You believe everything and you believe nothing. Like a child seeing magic tricks for the first time, you are impressed with each other. You are impressed with yourselves. And while it is my duty to guide you . . ." He paused, then said, "*I* am not impressed."

Spitting out words with a controlled fury, Gabriel added, "You speak of 'evolving' as if you are now the highest form of the concept. Humanity believes it has arrived at a glorious moment of significance. Yet you do not even comprehend the truth about yourselves. You have not *evolved*," he said with barely disguised disdain. "You have *devolved!*"

Haltingly, David spoke. "Gabriel, I do not intend to sound like I am disputing your words. I . . . I think we are just trying to understand what you are saying. For instance, not to be egotistical, as you said, but am I not presently living in the most advanced age humans have ever known?"

The archangel received the question and looked around the table. When he saw no one else was going to speak and realized they all agreed with the basis of David's question, Gabriel sighed heavily and said, "The question you are attempting to answer refers to restoring humanity to a pathway. You were correct in assuming that the word *restore* indicates humanity having been on the pathway before. But your belief, David Ponder, that mankind is experiencing an 'advanced age'—as you put it— causes me to despair of your ever finding the answer."

"Why?"

"Because if you are not even aware of the pathway to which the question is referring, how could you possibly hope to restore yourselves to it?"

"So what you are saying," Eric threw out, "is that we are not as advanced a civilization as we think we are."

"That is correct, Eric Erickson. There once existed a civilization on earth so advanced as to make you appear to be dull children in comparison. Their mathematics, engineering, architecture, and metallurgy were far beyond what you revere today. These were people of great understanding, great wisdom, and even greater faith."

"Why have we never heard of these people?" Eric asked.

"That is the same question you asked me once, David Ponder," Gabriel said. "Do you remember?"

"I do," David answered.

The archangel turned his attention back to Erickson. "You have no memory or cognitive knowledge of your history because most of your scientists work within a parameter of time that is far too narrow. A few of them, however, have begun to suspect that this society predated the Aztecs and Incas by more than thirty thousand of your years."

Winston couldn't help himself. "What indication is there of that?" he blurted.

"For you, Winston Churchill," Gabriel replied, "not much. You are too far removed from those people in terms of ability, capacity, wisdom, and time. The most intelligent members of your civilization are just now beginning to arrive at the point of recognizing and understanding the evidence they left of their existence."

"What evidence?" Joan asked.

"The obelisk of Luxor would be one," Gabriel said. "The massive stone is seventy-five feet tall and weighs more than four hundred tons. Your scientists today continue to argue about how a single piece that size could have been quarried and moved a hundred miles across the desert, and of course they still have no idea how it was set upright.

"Stonework creating entire cities in Bolivia, Egypt, and Peru surpass anything possible in today's world—even by your modern engineers. Granite blocks weighing hundreds of tons were transported over long distances after having been quarried to precisions—angles and edges—of less than the width of a human hair.

"The stones—some the size of your five-story buildings—were placed one on top of another over and over again until they reached the sky. These colossal blocks were aligned so perfectly that grout was not required. Today, only your diamond-tipped laser saws can approximate the precise specification of margin, but no machine or engineer on earth at this time can duplicate anything close in those size dimensions. It is a source of amusement to me that your scientists insist that these megalithic marvels rose from the dust of nomadic hunter-gatherers."

As those at the table listened in wonder, Gabriel continued. "Sophisticated astronomical alignments exist at sites all over the world. And while some of them have been discovered, most are not yet understood. The civilization that built these sites knew the exact circumference of Earth and chartered it into systems of measure around the world. Your mathematicians and engineers have now seen this in surviving buildings in South America, Europe, and Africa because the figures were incorporated into the architecture they left behind. And these equations were calculated perfectly. You, on the other hand, were only able to calculate these exact mathematical values after *Sputnik* circled Earth in 1957.

"Your scientists, with the benefit of satellite radar imaging, have now conceded the accuracy of ancient maps detailing the coastline of Antarctica. This was accomplished by others despite the fact that the location has been buried under thousands of feet of ice for millennia."

"Why are they gone?" Lincoln asked. "Why did that civilization disappear?"

"For the same reasons your civilization is in peril," Gabriel answered. "Arrogance, greed, selfishness, ungratefulness, loss of faith. But I might add, your people have managed to reach the precipice of the cliff in an astonishingly short time."

"Is there anything we can do to turn back?" David asked.

"Of course," Gabriel said. "That is why you are here. Until it is too late, it is never too late."

With no more questions forthcoming, the archangel said, "You have two more opportunities to answer the question." With those words, Gabriel stepped away from the table and across a hushed room.

Before he reached the door, however, to the disbelief of all, David called the archangel's name again. This time, he stopped and turned completely around. The archangel did not speak but focused his attention on David.

"Gabriel," David said in a voice that was soft in expression, yet audible to everyone in the theater, "you mentioned the moon. You said that there were clues about who made the moon in the first place. What clues? What did you mean?"

The archangel stood motionless, giving David the impression that he was composing his answer. Or perhaps, David thought, he wouldn't answer at all. But when Gabriel spoke, he did so in a manner that reminded David of his parents and how once, as a child, he had deeply disappointed his father.

"David Ponder," the archangel said carefully, "your civilization is enamored with the concept of chance. Chance. Luck. Randomness. A philosophy of contingency upon probabilities and possibilities. Chance—no assignable cause.

"You have embraced the idea of chance so completely that you have created entertainment to further the notion, and buildings and cities as monuments to the concept. You allow chance to steal your money and waste your time. Chance is given credit for the children you bear and the legacy you pass on to them. The idea of chance has made you greedy. Worse, it has made you arrogant. It has corrupted your minds, for now, many of you dare to attribute your world, your universe, your very existence . . . to 'chance.'

"Here is your clue, David Ponder: In a path of perfection that has existed since the second day, your Earth revolves 366 times during one orbit of the sun. Earth is exactly 366 percent larger than your moon. Conversely, your moon takes 27.32 days to orbit the Earth and is exactly 27.32 percent of the Earth's size. Your moon is 400 times closer to the Earth than it is to your sun and exactly 400 times smaller than the sun. As the moon turns, the speed of the lunar equator, by the way, is precisely 400 kilometers per hour."

Gabriel paused, then moved again toward the door, which was opening wide to meet him. Before he crossed the threshold, however, he turned, glanced around the room, and said, "What are the chances of that?"

CHAPTER 9

David sat down heavily as the room began to come to life around him. He looked at the others in turn and hoped they didn't see in his eyes what he felt. At that moment, David admitted to himself, he was terribly discouraged.

"Do not give in to the black dog," Churchill said, noting David's expression. When David questioned the comment, he explained. "I dealt with depression my entire life. I called it my black dog, for it seemed to follow me everywhere I went. The black dog wasn't always *on* me, wasn't always in sight, but I grew to find that he was ever nearby."

"Is that what I had?" Lincoln asked. "I never knew it was a black dog." The remark was only partially in jest, but it made David smile, and that is what the president had intended.

"I learned to be on my guard," Winston continued. "I never liked standing near the edge of a platform when an express train was passing through. I always stood far back and if possible got a pillar between the train and me. I wouldn't allow myself to stand by the side of a ship and look down into the water. A second's action would have ended everything. A few drops of desperation, a moment of incaution with my defenses down, and the black dog would have jumped me from behind."

Lincoln nodded. He told Winston he knew exactly how he felt, for he, too, had, been beset by depression.

"What did you do?" Joan asked. "How did you manage?"

Winston had his answer ready. "Never feed a black dog," he said. "They are always hungry, and the more one feeds a black dog, the closer its teeth get to one's own throat."

"How do you feed a black dog?" Eric asked.

"The better question, young man, would be, 'How do you starve a black dog?' For you see, bad questions only whet his appetite."

Eric looked around at the others. Only Lincoln was smiling as if he knew what Winston was talking about. "I don't get it," Eric finally said.

"The quality of one's answers," Winston explained, "can only be determined by the quality of one's questions. If you want good answers in your life, you must ask good questions.

"It is a fact that most of the talking we do on a daily basis is with ourselves. Whenever we ask something, our subconscious mind is determined to answer and immediately goes to work doing so." Winston thought for a beat and continued. "What I mean is that our subconscious works on whatever problem we give it to solve. Therefore, if one asks bad questions, one's mind descends to a state in which we work to furnish bad answers. Bad questions feed the black dog because they prompt negative thoughts. Then, of course, the black dog begins to feed on us."

Lincoln spoke up. "An example of a bad question from my own life," he said, "would be, 'Why can't I solve this problem between these people?' You see, when I asked that question, my mind began to think about all my deficiencies. *Well*, I would answer myself, *you can't solve this problem because you were not educated properly.* I worried about the way I looked. I talked to myself about the part of the country I was from, my accent, the mistakes I'd made in the past. All these depressing thoughts are answers to 'Why can't I . . . ?'

"Now, on the other hand, if I can manage to ask myself a *good* question, a question like, '*What is the best way* to solve this problem between these people?' at that moment, my mind goes to work on solutions. I have set my subconscious to think of best possibilities, and because of it, I am happier and more productive."

"I understand," Eric said. "So ask good questions, get good answers. You could even throw in other words to guide your subconscious, right? Like, 'What is the happiest, fastest, best way to solve this problem between these people?'"

"That's it," Winston said. "*Good* questions. That's how you starve the black dog."

"Then let me ask this," David said. "What is the fastest way to accurately answer the question before us?"

Though he was serious, David's question—a good one, he hoped—elicited chuckles from Churchill and Lincoln. The president had a quick response. "New blood will be the fastest way," he said. "New counsel. We are tired of listening to each other. I believe it is time to call another Traveler."

With all agreed, David stood, quieting the theater, and said, "The summit requests the assistance of a Traveler."

149

Every eye in the theater was directed toward the middle aisle behind Lincoln, Joan, and Eric. A large man had risen from the shadows—the sixth row—and was already making his way down the steps. His hair was dark, curly, and almost shoulder length. A band of braided gold wrapped around his head, holding his hair away from his face.

He wore sandals and a leather loincloth that stopped just above his knees. His shirt, also of leather, was sleeveless and studded with bronze and silver. Coiled around the deeply tanned skin of his muscular upper arms were thick bands of gold. The man's fingers were bare of rings, but his wrists were encased in solid pieces of polished bronze.

He was one of the most incredible sights David had ever seen. The man carried himself in a manner that while not threatening was certainly imposing. Everyone at the table stood as the man approached, but oddly, no one made a move to shake his hand or greet him in any traditional manner. He strode directly to the head of the table and said, "You may be seated."

Curious, David thought to himself as he sat down. Churchill and Lincoln also took their chairs after raising their eyebrows to each other in unspoken words. When this whole thing started, they had noticed immediately that the appointed leader of their group, David Ponder, had not chosen the head of the table—the power position—from which to conduct the summit. Instead, he had chosen to sit with everyone else.

Churchill and Lincoln had recognized the humble

maneuver because it was one they also had often employed. Now, though, they seated themselves without rancor, for both suspected the identity of the new arrival. Eric, on the other hand, remained standing for a moment longer, as if to communicate to the man that he was not intimidated and would do as he pleased. David was already seated, and of the five, only the Maid of Orleans did not sit down.

Her sword had been in front of her since she arrived. But now Joan took it up and, with it lying flat on her upturned palms, walked toward the man who had assumed the head of the table. He watched as she approached him without expression and made no move except to turn in her direction. When she was in front of him, Joan kneeled, raising the sword above her bowed head.

The man took it, and as she looked up, he nodded to her. Joan returned to her chair, and only then did the man place the sword on the table—this time in front of himself—and sit down in the place he had chosen.

When she had returned to her chair, Joan noticed Eric, who was seated to her left, staring as if she had lost her mind. Though he had not asked, Joan felt the need to explain. "I am not a woman to him. I am a warrior. And a king never comes to a council table with armed warriors. He does not have his men with him here. Therefore, by tradition, my weapon must be presented to the king himself."

"King?" Eric said. "What king?"

Never taking her eyes off the man about whom she was

speaking and aware that he was growing impatient with what he considered Eric's ill manners, Joan whispered, "The king who slew the giant as a boy. King David."

That information managed to open Eric's eyes *and* close his mouth. Taking advantage of the silence, the king looked at David Ponder and said, "You may begin."

To his credit, David did not say any of the things that came to his mind. He tried to remember that King David was the only one at the table so far who probably didn't know who any of the others were. However, after the lecture about egotistical behavior they'd just been given a few minutes ago, he did want to call Gabriel back in and ask if he had ever noticed this guy! *I suppose I am fortunate,* David thought, *that the king didn't assign me another name.* But David had known for a long time how to deal with people like this. After all, that's why he had chosen the middle chair when Winston had appeared.

"Sir," David said to the king, "as I am sure you already know, my very name is an honor to your legacy. We appreciate so much having you here. Your wisdom will be a touchstone for this summit as we seek the answer that has thus far been beyond our meager minds."

Lincoln suppressed a grin from across the table as David poured it on, but Winston, sitting next to him, hissed, "Oh, for God's own sake, why don't you give the man a massage?" And before David could do anything about it, Winston added, "Let me do this," and addressed the king himself.

"Sir," he said, "we are honored by your presence, but time is of the essence. I am certain that you already consider this summit to be similar to the councils you held with Israel, Judah, and your neighbors on the east bank of the Jordan River as you were establishing your kingdom. While we are assembled as such, engaged in an historic and monumental task, I assume you would have us communicate as you yourself suggested so long ago, as equals. It worked when you first proposed it, and I, for one, defer to your wisdom and leadership again."

Winston looked around the table with eyes wide, as if to say, *Come on, people. Work with me here.* And they did. Everyone agreed loudly. "Oh, what insight! If only we had thought of that!"

As Lincoln, Joan, and Eric were backing Churchill's proposal, David leaned in to Winston and quietly said, "Thank you. Well done."

"No challenge, my boy," Winston replied. "It's just like dealing with the French."

As they got down to business, Lincoln remembered to ask, "Is there a particular motion the theater makes through you at this time, sir?"

"Yes," the king responded. Addressing David, he said, "My son Solomon was seated with me. He sends greetings to you."

"Thank you," David responded and looked up into the dark from where the king had come, but he could not see Solomon.

King David continued. "As we have discussed possible solutions, Solomon has held fast to his conviction, an answer with which most of us now agree. I certainly believe it to be the answer but, because of our equal stature at this moment, will allow discussion."

"Oh, how noble of you, Your Majesty," Winston blurted out, earning himself a reproving glare from Lincoln.

"Thank you, sir," the president said immediately. "What is the solution your wise son proposes?"

"Exert self-discipline," King David said. "Control over one's self. Heart, muscle, and mind."

"That could be it," Winston said. "That very well could be it."

"The other three—hope, wisdom, and courage," Eric said cautiously, "certainly fit into self-discipline as a larger category."

"Why do you believe self-discipline to be the answer?" Joan asked the king.

"Because everything I ever accomplished in my life was because of it."

"I'd love to hear some of those specifics," Lincoln said, "if you don't mind."

Thoughtful for a minute, King David smiled and seemed to relax for the first time since he had arrived. "My first lesson in self-discipline," he began, "was the one I carried with me for the rest of my days. In fact, whenever I needed to remind myself of this mighty principle, I had this to touch, to feel, to remember. For you see, I really did carry it with me for the rest of my days."

As King David had spoken, he pulled from inside his shirt a fist-sized, wadded-up mass of leather cord. When he shook it out, everyone at the table widened their eyes, but Joan reached across Eric and held out her hand. "May I?" she asked.

"Of course." The king smiled and placed it in her hand.

Joan stood and stretched the object to its full length, which was about the span of her arm. It was a simple construction—two leather cords, both tied at one end to a leather piece about the size of Joan's palm. "You still have it," she said in awe, and the king—once a shepherd boy—smiled and nodded.

It was the sling with which he had slain Goliath of Gath, the giant, champion of the Philistine army. The story was familiar to all of them, and as they passed the relic around the table, they asked questions like excited children.

Patiently, the king answered every one of them. "Yes," he said, "this is *the* very sling. Yes, I chose five stones from the brook. No, I used only one. Yes, I really did take his sword and cut off his head with it." And on and on until the sling had come back to King David.

At last, he laid the sling on the hilt of Joan's sword and said, "As many times as I've told that story, I am amazed at the people who assume that to have been the first time I ever used the sling."

"What do you mean?" asked Eric, who was now as much in awe of King David as the others.

"Before the giant, I killed a lion and a bear. Both were after my father's sheep. But before the lion and the bear," the king said with a teasing smile, "I must have slain ten thousand rocks and trees!"

Eric laughed politely, but he knew the point. David, the shepherd boy, had practiced with the sling for months and years. There was a reason he had been able to kill a lion and a bear. And there was a reason that it took only one shot to fell the giant.

"It takes self-discipline to practice, because practice is rarely exciting. But I understood the principle at an early age. Exerting self-discipline is merely a process by which you remember what you really want. You see, I did not want to practice. What I *really wanted* was to be proficient with the sling. Therefore, I learned to discipline myself to practice on targets—rocks and trees—for hours every day.

"What do you really want? That is the question that fuels a person to a strong discipline that can only be administered to himself by himself. And success in any endeavor where self-discipline is involved boils down to this question: can you make yourself do something you don't particularly want to do in order to get a result you *would* like to have?"

"That is it," Eric said to everyone. "That is absolutely the best I've ever heard it described."

Then the king spoke seriously. "In my life, I learned self-discipline, and I knew that the principle yielded great reward. But I feel that before we continue, I must speak to you about the other side of the coin. Yes, self-discipline leads to reward. But a lack of self-discipline does not always mean that *nothing* happens. A *lack* of self-discipline can lead to disaster."

While the others waited, King David drew in a great breath

and let it out slowly before he began. When he did, it was with great introspection and sadness. "It is true that I have known great victories . . . great success. It is also true that these successes were almost without exception rooted in self-discipline."

Here, the king paused, seeming to see in the distant past something that pained him greatly. "Unfortunately, I also know great failure." Pausing again, he added, "Failure of a most personal, horrible kind." Looking at David, he said, "Curiously, other than my name, my kingdom, my son, and the story of Goliath, most of my life on earth was lived with only a few human beings knowing my deepest secrets. Upon my arrival in this place, however, imagine my shock when I found that my darkest deeds were recorded and passed down in written form. You have already heard what I am about to discuss, and the facts do not flatter my memory. But if we are to explore self-discipline—especially the lack of it—the telling of this story is relevant."

The king breathed deeply again and began. "One evening when I should have been somewhere else, I saw a woman—a beautiful woman—and wanted her. Her name was Bathsheba. She was married to a man in my army. He was a Hittite. His name was Uriah. This I knew and sent for her anyway." He looked at the others and added, "I was the king. Bathsheba had little choice in the matter.

"After she became pregnant, I sent word to my captain that Uriah should be placed on the front line of battle. Where he was killed. Where he was murdered. By me.

"I won't take the time to share my guilt, my grief, my punishment, or my repentance. The point of this story for you, at this time, is to recognize the choices involved in this principle. The most reliable evidence for the power of self-discipline is to observe the wreckage caused by its absence."

After a moment of contemplation, Churchill said, "I think we can all point out choices in our lives that were bereft of discipline—self-discipline or any other kind. I must say, however, that it was self-discipline that enabled me to beat off the black dog over and over again."

"How so?" Eric asked.

"You tell him," Winston said to Lincoln. "If everything I've read about you is true, you know the answer as well as I."

Lincoln said, "It's true. Depression—what the prime minister deems the black dog—was a common state of mind for me until I learned that I could discipline myself to feel differently."

Eric gave the president a skeptical look. "Okay . . . ," he said.

"I have come to believe that cheerfulness in most cheerful people is simply the result of self-discipline. During the first half of my adulthood, when I got depressed, which was often, I responded by taking naps, avoiding people, brooding, and thinking about how depressed I was. Most of the habits I developed in response to my depression simply made my depression worse and extended the life span of my desperate feeling."

"You were feeding the black dog," Eric said with a quick grin at Winston.

"Exactly," Lincoln replied. "But somewhere along the line, I realized that there were certain people whose company amused me. I realized that there were certain places where, when I visited, my spirits soared. I realized that certain music made me happy, certain books made me laugh, and that a brisk walk brought a smile to my face.

"And so I learned to discipline myself to walk instead of sleep, to enjoy the company of certain people instead of brooding alone, to read good books and listen to happy music instead of reflecting sorrowfully or desperately on my feelings of depression."

Eric started to speak when Lincoln stopped him. "Wait," he said. "I know your objection. You want to say, 'But the problem is that when I am depressed, I don't *feel* like doing those things!'

"Of course you don't," the president continued. "And that is exactly why we are talking about self-discipline! Think about what the king said just a few moments ago. He said, 'What do you want?' Well, *I* wanted to be happy."

Lincoln continued. "Then the king said, 'Can you make yourself do something you don't particularly want to do in order to get a result that you want?' You know, when I am depressed, I can promise you that I do not want to see other people or read amusing books or listen to happy music. I just want to *be* happy. But I have learned that I *can* discipline myself to do some things I don't particularly want to do—smile, walk, visit a cheerful friend—to get a result I *do* want.

"Remember, the king did not want to practice with the sling; he only wanted to kill a giant. The giant in my life was depression. I did not want to practice my smile either. I only wanted to kill my giant. You see?"

"I do," Eric said, "I really do. And I don't mean to be obstinate with this question, but what if I am just not that kind of person?"

"I have this one," Winston said, raising his hand. "My boy," he began, "if you are not that kind of person, then you must become another kind."

Eric gave Churchill an exasperated look and was about to say something when the prime minister cut him off. "I am not teasing you," he said. "Think! If you are poor, you work to become financially comfortable. If you are weak, you discipline yourself with exercise. Why? Because you don't like the way you look or feel.

"In the same way, we are absolutely capable of disciplining our minds to change who, what, and how we are. For many years, when I was depressed, I acted depressed! At some point, I came to understand that how I behaved—how I acted—ultimately controlled how I felt. So I disciplined myself to act in the manner in which I wanted to feel."

Joan said, "I am not certain that I am capable of acting in a manner contrary to that which I feel."

"Ha!" Winston shouted and pointed to Eric sitting beside her. "He knew better than to say that. When Eric felt fear in Himmler's office, he acted confidently. When he felt anger as his friend was shot before his very eyes, he acted nonchalantly. This man had to act in a manner contrary to that which he felt. If he had acted like he felt, he would have been killed!

"Therefore, I would put to you, fair Maid, that there were many times in your life when you walked from an angry confrontation to a meeting that required you to act in a manner contrary to how you were feeling at that moment.

"Self-discipline begins with the mastery of your mind. As the king so eloquently stated, you must remember what you want. It is a thought process. You *can* learn to control how you think. If you don't control how you think, you cannot control how you act. Self-discipline is the bridge between what you are and what you wish to become. And unless you change how you think and how you act, you will always be what you are."

"Rule your mind, or it will rule you," King David agreed. Adding a comment that was no surprise to the president and the prime minister, he said, "I, too, suffered from periods of what you call depression."

Lincoln only nodded politely, but Winston couldn't help himself. "No!" he said in mock horror. "I'd never have guessed."

As a king, David was probably not accustomed to sarcasm of any kind, much less from someone so apparently unafraid of him as Winston seemed to be. But to his credit, the king appeared to be amused by this chubby old man. Smiling at Churchill, David asked, "How would *you* know whether I was ever depressed?"

Winston looked around the table at everyone. "He's joking,

right?" he asked. Then to the king, he said, "Dear sir, I am an avid reader of your most famous work. The Psalms are brilliant, of course, and I always found them perfectly inspirational for—in particular—me.

"Now . . . how did I know whether or not you were depressed? Good heavens, sir, have you read what you wrote? The Psalms are a veritable course study in depression. You're happy. You're sad. You're ecstatic. You're miserable. God loves you. He's forgotten you. And one might find all that in a single psalm. You make *me* look positively stable!"

To everyone's relief, the king laughed heartily and was not only joined by those at the table, but the entire theater as well. "All I can say in my defense," the king finally said, "is that perhaps those feelings are more common than I had realized."

"After my travel," David Ponder said, "I became a voracious reader of biographies. In reading about the lives of great people—yours included—I found that the first great victory most of them won was over themselves. That was especially true of their emotions. All the other great things that happened in their lives came after they mastered self-discipline. But it is a subtle thing and not often discussed. Everyone is always looking for different reasons to explain why they failed and why others succeeded.

"In addition—while I am on the subject of great people—it seems obvious to me that self-sacrifice is a form of self-discipline. When one's actions reflect his or her own interests, the results are never good for the family, the team, the corporation, the country—or whatever it is that person is supposed to represent."

"True," Lincoln inserted. "I have often observed legislators voting a certain way to benefit their state, knowing full well that the vote is detrimental to the country as a whole. When we say or do things we do not believe—things we know in our heart are not in the best interests of the many—to keep a job or position of power, it is the worst kind of lie. Elected officials, I believe, should pay particular attention to the form of self-discipline known as self-sacrifice."

"Maybe this *is* the answer," Joan said. "Self-discipline."

"What else could it be?" the king asked.

"I don't know," Winston said, "but I already asked myself that three other times."

"Self-discipline is an act of investment," Eric thought aloud. "It requires us to invest today's actions for tomorrow's results. I'm just saying that exhibiting self-discipline is something that would restore humanity to a pathway toward . . . you know."

"Self-discipline on display marks one as a person to follow," King David said. "Self-discipline strengthens the heart and mind. Dignity, honor, wealth, influence, authority—all are products of this one principle."

The king grew pensive. "When I disciplined myself as a shepherd . . . when I disciplined myself as a warrior and as a young ruler. When I disciplined myself as a father . . ." He paused, seemingly lost in memories. "When I disciplined myself, my life's results were predictable. I killed a giant. I led armies." He looked to his right and up into the theater. "I was a good father when I disciplined myself."

"But what is in our power to do is also in our power *not* to do. If we do not discipline ourselves, the world will be allowed to do it for us. When I failed my men with the murder of Uriah . . . when I failed my family . . . my world fell apart. My armies divided. My sons rebelled.

"Yes, I repented and received forgiveness, but the consequences of my actions lasted the rest of my life. I deem the man who overcomes his desires more courageous than he who conquers his enemies. The most difficult triumph is over one's own self."

After each looked at the others for a moment or two, Eric asked, "Are we ready?" They all looked to David Ponder.

"I think so," he said cautiously. "I think so." When no one disagreed or had anything to add, David stood. In a strong voice, he said, "I am ready with the answer."

As Gabriel entered the room, David Ponder leaned across the table to Lincoln and whispered, "Sir . . . Mr. President . . . I would like you to present this answer—*the* answer—to Gabriel." As the surprise registered on Lincoln's face, David added, "Please, sir. Please . . ."

By the time David had made his request and sat down, the archangel was standing in his usual place at the end of the table. "David Ponder," he said, "I look forward to hearing the conclusion of this previous discussion. The wisdom of the king added some perspective, I am certain. And perhaps *our* time together during the break was of some small benefit."

"Yes, Gabriel," David answered. "If you don't mind, President Lincoln will speak for us this time."

The archangel signaled his approval, and Lincoln stood. "Sir," the president began, "previous to this opportunity, three times we have settled on and presented to you what turned out to be erroneous answers. We do believe though, sir, that those discussions have led us to what you intended all along. For the answer we present not only encompasses but empowers the restoration of hope, an active search for wisdom, and an obvious display of courage."

Everyone in the room was entranced by the president's easy manner and the logical way he was spontaneously delivering their answer to Gabriel. With both hands grasping the lapels of his suit coat, Lincoln wound to the conclusion. "Sir, we have determined that while our answer is a principle that is difficult for mankind to grasp and accomplish, it is what humanity needs to restore itself to the pathway toward successful civilization.

"Yes, Gabriel . . . while the answer we offer is demanding and sometimes painful, it is necessary. Therefore, we have determined that humanity must suffer one of two things: the pain of self-discipline or the pain of regret. We intend to make that choice for humanity. 'Exhibit self-discipline,' sir, is our answer."

The president had not broken eye contact with Gabriel the entire time he was speaking, but now, having finished, he looked at the others for support. Their faces told the story.

They were very hopeful. The answer was logical, and the way Lincoln had expressed it to the archangel sounded perfect.

But as good as it sounded—as logical as it was—the answer was wrong.

As Lincoln sat back down, Gabriel informed them of their error in his usual fashion. He commended President Lincoln on his presentation, reminded David of the one opportunity remaining to answer the question, and left the room.

Around the table, only King David appeared to be staggered by the defeat. The others were taking it in stride. "Wow," Eric said to Lincoln. "You were great. Even if the answer was wrong, I'd have had to give it to you for how you spoke."

"Excellent job," Winston said. "I'm with him."

Lincoln smiled ruefully and said, "I am not worried. I never got anything right until my last try anyway." He rubbed his hands on the table and, changing the subject, said, "I've been in love with this piece—the chairs too—since the first time I saw it. Beautiful work."

"You've seen this table previously?" Winston asked. "On what occasion?"

Lincoln shrugged. "I've had dinner at this table before. Twice."

"Really?" Winston said with a bit of awe in his voice. Rubbing his own hands on the beveled edge, he mused, "It really is beautiful work."

"It was handmade," Lincoln said with a twinkle in his eye. "Of course, you know, the Boss's Son is a carpenter."

CHAPTER 10

The theater hummed with Travelers grouped in the aisles, some gatherings spilling out onto the floor. All were careful, however, not to get too close to the table. As David looked around him, he could tell that they were communicating with an urgency that had not been evident before. Each group seemed to have emissaries who walked from gathering to gathering, monitoring what was being discussed and keeping the others informed.

For the first time, David spotted Anne Frank, who was passionately delivering her opinion to the group that included Golda Meir and Teddy Roosevelt. It took all the willpower David could muster not to run over to Anne and hug her, but restrained by the rules, he did not.

While he watched that same group, a man in a houndstooth hat, whom David recognized immediately as Bear Bryant, caught his eye and gave him a thumbs-up. When the old football coach held up four fingers and smiled, David laughed out loud and returned the thumbs-up. David knew the coach was telling him to stay strong—that the fourth quarter was his!

Mentally returning to his own group at the table, David saw the discussion was well under way. "It is just *not*!" Winston was saying irritably to Eric.

"Fine," Eric said holding up his hands. "Fine. I'm just saying we should explore everything."

"We have *explored* compassion," Winston growled, "and that is not the answer!"

Eric rolled his eyes, and King David saw the reaction. "Can I borrow your sling for a minute?" Winston asked, causing the king to laugh.

"Eric," Lincoln said, "I think we have to look beyond this type of answer. Think of what we have put forward so far. Hope, wisdom, courage, and self-discipline—"

In the breath that he took to continue, Eric jumped in. "Sir," he said, "I totally understand. I just don't know where else to go with this."

"I missed something here," David said. "I apologize, and I'm sorry for making you backtrack, but . . ."

"All the answers are alike," Joan said.

"Yes," Lincoln confirmed, "while they all somehow appear to fit as a piece of the other's puzzle, perhaps that significance is not as pronounced as we assumed. In any case, 'compassion' seems to be another answer in the same vein as hope, courage, and the others. And we are obviously adding the second word when we present our solution to Gabriel, though I don't feel in any of the answers a second word was necessary. In any case, all the answers we are putting forth *do* seem to be the same."

"I agree," Eric said. "Same for 'love' or 'humility' or any number of other virtues."

"I just believe that we must go in an entirely different direction," Winston said a bit petulantly. "I believe it strongly."

"Yes," Eric whispered to the king and rolled his eyes again, "we know." King David thought this was terribly funny.

"Shh," Joan said and swatted Eric with her hand under the table. Trying not to smile, she kept her attention on the others.

David sighed. "But what direction?" he said blankly. I feel further away from the answer now than I did when we started."

Suddenly, there was a burst of applause and excited voices from one of the groups in the theater. Behind David and Winston, Benjamin Franklin hurried from that gathering to the one in the next aisle. After a brief moment of communication, that group also became animated.

As everyone at the table watched in amazement, whatever had sprung from the Franklin gathering made its way around the theater. Again and again, they heard clapping and "Yes!" being proclaimed along with other expressions of affirmation. Finally, the whole theater turned their attention to those at the table and applauded loudly.

David scanned the room. He saw Anne again, and this time, she saw him. Her eyes were excited and her head bobbed up and down at him as she waved to him and clapped with everyone else. Christopher Columbus was standing in his chair, cheering wildly, and almost fell onto Sir Edmund Hillary, who steadied him and ordered him to the floor.

Paul Harvey, on the first row, waved, and when he had

David's eye, pointed to an older black gentleman standing beside him. The man was conservatively dressed in a suit with a vest and bow tie. He was also clapping, but not quite as enthusiastically as the others. As the applause began to diminish, David noticed a large part of the audience looking toward that very man. As they all sat down, Booker T. Washington reached over from the second row and patted him on the shoulder. He turned, smiled graciously, and accepted what appeared to be Dr. Washington's congratulations.

With the crowd quiet at last, they all turned expectantly to David, who looked across the table to Lincoln and questioned him with an expression. The president smiled and said, "It appears, my friend, that the people have spoken."

"They have found the answer," Joan said excitedly.

Eric, a bit more cynical than the rest, tempered her enthusiasm. "They have found what they *think* is the answer," he said. "You might remember that we have accomplished that much four times already."

"No, this is it," Winston crowed. David wasn't sure if Churchill really believed that or was simply disagreeing for the fun of it.

When King David pointed directly at the black man on the first row, everyone at the table cringed. Had no one ever told the king it was impolite to point? And who, they wondered, would? No one, it turned out. He announced, "It was the Ethiopian. He discovered the answer."

Eric leaned over and said, "Ah . . . I don't think he is Ethiopian."

"Of course he is," the king replied. "They have a reputation for brilliance."

"As far as I am concerned," Lincoln said, "I believe it time to call our last associate. Are you as anxious as I to hear what they have agreed upon?"

"I am," David responded. "Anyone else have anything to offer before I do this?" No one did, so he stood and for the fifth time—the final time—said, "The summit requests the assistance of a Traveler."

For some reason, David had been looking at the black gentleman when he made the call and was fascinated to see the man frown, cock his head, and turn to look briefly at Dr. Washington behind him. Then he stood up.

David was not at all prepared for the response the gentleman received from the theater when he moved toward the table. The Travelers in the audience all stood up with him. Whistling and clapping as he walked the short distance to where he would now be sitting, they were wholeheartedly showing their appreciation for this man and their approval of the choice.

"That man changed the world," Winston said as they all came out of their chairs to join the ovation.

"Who is he?" David asked.

"That, my friend," Winston said, "is one of the greatest human beings to have ever walked the planet. That is George Washington Carver."

Carver appeared to be past seventy years of age, and his close-cropped hair was almost completely gray. The green bow tie he wore marked him as an intellectual, David thought, but it was the way he carried himself that set him apart. He looked comfortable in his skin. It would have been a hard thing to describe, but the way he shook hands with everyone at the table, the manner in which he had acknowledged the ovation, and his humble smile all added up to a man who was at ease with himself and those around him.

"Everyone obviously loves you," David said as they all sat down. The old gentleman took the only chair left, the one to the right of David and on the end, next to the king.

"They are very kind," he said looking up into the theater. Shaking his head in amazement, he added, "I've got to tell you, I am flat-out excited to be sitting here!" At the table, they all laughed appreciatively, but before anyone could say anything, the man leaned around David to speak to Winston. "Mr. Prime Minister," he smiled broadly, "I have something for *you*."

What could it be? David wondered, as Carver reached first into one pants pocket, then with the other hand, reached into the pocket on the opposite side. Holding up an object between the thumb and forefinger of his right hand, Carver said, "Do you believe it?"

Winston reached out to receive the gift. It was a 1909 Lincoln penny—just like the one he had given the president earlier. "Oh my!" Winston said. "Are you certain you want me to have this?"

"Yes," Carver answered almost bursting with excitement. "Look at this." In his left hand, he held up *another* 1909 penny. "I am sorry for the rest of you folks," he said with a chuckle, "but now that the president has one and the prime minister has one *again*—this one's mine!"

To Lincoln, he said, "Mr. President, I was born in 1864 or '65. Not exactly sure, but it was right around the time your war ended. My natural mama and daddy were slaves. So when you signed the Emancipation Proclamation, sir, you emancipated *me*.

"Now, it's a long, crazy story, and I don't want to bore you good people with it, but a white couple—Moses and Susan Carver—not only saved my life when Quantrill's Raiders kidnapped my family, but they adopted me.

"It was Mama Carver who gave me this penny when it came out in 1909. There were a lot of them around then, of course, but she told me, 'George, that man was *your* president, and he was a wonderful man.' Mama said that I was to remember you with gratefulness in my heart and this penny in my pocket.

"Anyhow," he continued, "that little copper picture of you that I just gave to the prime minister was one I got on my own not too long after Mama gave me this first one. I wanted two of 'em. A penny in each pocket, don't you know, just seems to give a man some balance!" He laughed, and the others laughed with him.

David had a little deeper understanding of the ovation

from the audience now. It wasn't just that Carver had helped with whatever answer they were about to hear. Everyone loved this man. *Odd*, David mused. *The greatest figures in the history of the world, all of them together in one room, and a former slave is the most popular person in the place.*

"Thank you from the bottom of my heart, Dr. Carver," Winston said, holding up the penny before dramatically placing it into his suit-coat pocket. "I shall now be able to treasure this coin as a remembrance of two people. Again, thank you."

"Dr. Carver?" David said, "I am eager to hear what you said over there that has gotten everyone so excited.

The others at the table added their encouragement, and Carver began. "Well, I can't remember who it was, but as we were talking, someone remarked that all these virtues we have been offering up as 'the answer' were the components of greatness. All I said was, 'No . . . these are merely the components of character. It is a person's *character* that will determine greatness.'"

No one at the table said anything. Eyebrows were raised, and they looked at one another as if waiting for someone to disagree. But no one did.

"Building character," Lincoln said softly. "Of course. Why does this seem so crystal clear now? But think of it: character—not hope, but character—makes a complete person."

"Wisdom develops in quiet places," Winston said. "Character is formed in the swirling storms that are human life."

Eric nodded. "It makes sense. Courage generally requires bravery of the mind as it risks the body. Character requires bravery of the soul as it risks everything."

"What do you want?" King David said. "Remember? That is the question of self-discipline. And the discipline of desire is the very basis of building character."

Carver smiled. "'It is not circumstances, but character alone that makes the man.' 'Twas Dr. Booker T. Washington who said those words. Told me that on a hot day in Tuskegee, Alabama." Thinking for a bit, he added, "See now, circumstances come and go . . . they ebb and flow. Not only is it not circumstances that make the man, but no *change* in circumstances can repair a defect in a man's character."

"Character isn't something you are born with and can't change," Joan said. "It is something you are *not* born with. Character is a thing we alone are responsible to form . . . to build. And we build it with hope, wisdom, courage, and self-discipline."

"Does adversity build character?" Eric asked.

"No," King David responded quickly.

Everyone looked at the king and waited for him to explain his answer. When he did not, Eric said, "Okaaay."

Lincoln chuckled and offered, "If I may . . . Certainly, I would never compare myself to the king, but"—he nodded toward Winston—"I believe the prime minister and I, having occupied positions of authority, have some idea of the mindset from which that last answer originated."

Winston blinked slowly and nodded once as an acknowl-edgment of the president's words. Lincoln continued, "Does adversity build character? I agree that it does not. Almost all people can stand adversity of one sort or another. If you want to test a person's character, give him power.

"Now, since we are concerning ourselves here with the very future of humanity, let me add one thing more. Power corrupts. Trust me on this. And because power corrupts, humanity's need for those in power to be of high charac-ter increases as the importance of the position of leadership increases.

"We are discussing character, correct? Not intelligence. Some of the most intelligent leaders in history have brought disaster to their nations because intelligence is powerless to modify character. Great leadership is a product of great char-acter. And this is why character matters."

Winston looked to Carver. "Sir," he said, "I have seen the statue and plaque that exists of you in London." To the others, he remarked, "Dr. Carver is an elected member of the Royal Society for Encouragement of Arts—the world's oldest scientific organization." Back to Carver, he went on. "There are statues of you in Russia, India, and all over the African continent."

Remembering more he wanted to say, Winston addressed those at the table again. "This man lived in a tiny apartment on the campus of Tuskegee Institute. Franklin and Eleanor told me this next bit, by the way. In that tiny apartment, the crown prince of Sweden came to stay. Not to visit for an afternoon, but to stay for a week! Mahatma Gandhi came all the way from India; bypassed Washington, D.C.; and went directly to Tuskegee. Henry Ford, Thomas Edison—these men and many more made their way to that apartment. There they spent the night, they ate their meals . . . all to be in the presence of this man."

"Dr. Carver, sir," Winston said shifting in his chair again, "I don't know if you are even aware of this, but there exists in Missouri, the state of your birth, a national monument in your honor. This, sir, was the first national monument in the history of the United States established for a person of your color. But color has never been relevant. The race you represent is the human race. And we are the greater for having you a part of it."

Churchill's oration was typical of him. The words were formed beautifully and enunciated with passion. The subject of the discourse—George Washington Carver—was as awed as everyone else in the room. The prime minister's ability to communicate was beyond extraordinary. Which was why they all laughed when Winston looked around and added at the end, "He did a lot of things with plants!"

When the laughter died down, Joan asked, "What did you do with plants, Dr. Carver? I'm sorry I don't know, but I am curious."

"Oh, dear child," he said kindly, "there wasn't much to it, really. I was just trying to help some farmers and ended up figuring a few extra ways to use what was already there."

"Oh come on," Eric snorted good-naturedly. "I know a little about you myself." To Joan he said, "He created almost three hundred uses for the peanut and around about a hundred for the sweet potato. All those things are still being used today. Crop rotation, soybeans into plastic, cotton into paving blocks, wood chips into synthetic marble . . ."

Eric paused and thought for a moment, brightened, and said, "Got it. Listen to this. This quote is carved into the George Washington Carver monument: 'He could have added fortune to fame, but caring for neither, he found happiness and honor in being helpful to the world.'" Popping his hand on the top of the table, Eric added, "That, my friends, is character."

"That, my friends," Carver said with a chuckle, "is enough about me."

Ignoring Carver for the moment, Winston stared hard at Eric and asked, "That last part . . . the quote. How did you remember that?"

Eric replied with a grin. "Mr. Prime Minister, you aren't the only person who has read books. And as for remembering, I have 'total recall' with regard to maps, plans, anything written down. Remembering things is what I do."

"Hmm. Yes," Winston said darkly. Grinning suddenly and jabbing a thumb toward Carver, he said, "Quite a reputation, eh?"

Carver frowned slightly. "If I may . . . ," he said. Noting his expression, they all grew attentive. "While I appreciate so much your kind words, I feel I must insert here a reminder that it is not *reputation* about which one should be concerned. It is character. I cannot stress this enough.

"What must humanity do, individually and collectively, to restore itself to the pathway toward successful civilization? The answer, I believe we agree, is that we must build character. We must build character in our children. We must build character in ourselves. We must insist upon the presence of character in our leadership—insist upon it! Does not history show us that our leaders are a critical part—perhaps *the* critical part—of humanity's journey on any pathway that has ever been traveled? One person leads us upon one pathway, while another leader might choose an entirely different direction.

"So please, let us remember that it is character—not reputation—that is the answer. If we build character, our reputations will take care of themselves."

"True," Lincoln said. "Reputation is merely what others think you might be. Character is what we really are. Character is what a man *is* in the dark."

David said, "I am excited about this. I think we have it. But before we move to close this up, let's talk a bit more about character itself. How is it determined? How is it built?"

Joan said, "I believe that *my* character—whatever that may be—is a result of the wisdom I have sought, the people with whom I associate, how I choose to spend my time, and the discipline I impose upon my attitude." After pausing to think, she added, "I think my character is the sum total of my habits."

"Nothing shows a person's character more than his habits," King David agreed.

"The things that amuse a person reveal much," Eric tossed in. "What you laugh at, what you cry about, what disgusts you or doesn't . . . I am telling you," he said, "that the way people see the world and react to their fellow man is a huge indication of their character."

They all looked at each other, and from the audience, a smattering of applause became a roar. Everyone at the table smiled in relief and anticipation. When the applause died away, David looked at everyone. "This is it," he said. "Does anyone have anything to add before we call Gabriel?"

"I think you've done a marvelous job," Winston said. "You've hit the right note leading this bunch." To the others, he asked, "Don't you think?"

"Absolutely," Joan said. "And thank *you*, sir," she added to Carver.

Accepting Joan's gratitude, Carver deflected it. "Certainly, this was a group effort. I changed nothing . . . just added a small piece to the puzzle." He looked to the audience, and as he did, David stood and applauded those in the theater seats. The others—even the king—joined in to show appreciation for their contribution.

"I am ready with the answer," David said a few minutes later.

As the door opened and Gabriel entered, David asked Carver if he would do the honor of making the final presentation. But no, as was his wont, the humble man deferred. "You do this, David," he said. "We have all been a part of it, but we want you to deliver the remedy to this challenge." The others smiled and nodded their agreement.

Gabriel said nothing at all. He simply went to the place where he had received the answers before. This time, however, David felt differently. It did not unnerve him that the archangel was silent. He was not unsettled by the situation or the enormity of the words he was about to utter. To begin, David repeated what he had said four times already. "Gabriel," David said, "I am ready with the answer."

With no other discernible move, the archangel simply and slowly nodded. It was David's signal to begin. And so he did.

"Gabriel," he began, "as a group, we appreciate the opportunity to have gathered here together. Our unsuccessful efforts in answering the question with which we were tasked ultimately led us not only to the answer itself, but to greater knowledge to benefit humanity as a whole. The previous solutions we explored—while incorrect—did succeed in bringing us to what we now recognize as the answer."

David relaxed. Gabriel was nodding now. It was slight, but David saw the archangel's gesture, and as he spoke, David's confidence increased. "It was an exploration of hope, Gabriel, that allowed us to begin this quest with great energy and expectation.

"We sought wisdom, and our hope began to take greater shape. The understanding we gained about the necessity of courage moved hope and wisdom into action—and a broader search for where the true answer might lie. And though discouraged, our own exhibition of self-discipline kept us in the race long enough to develop"—David lifted his chin—"what humanity also needs to develop. And that would be . . . character.

"So the answer, sir, is that humanity, with its attention focused to 'building character,' will restore itself to the pathway toward successful civilization."

It only took a moment for the archangel to smile, and when he did, cheers erupted from every corner of the room.

CHAPTER 11

The celebration extended into the audience. David turned to shake hands with Winston, who was fumbling for a cigar. Carver stood, looking across the table and up into the audience. He waved at Dr. Washington, who had both fists in the air and a victorious grin.

Joan formally shook hands with Eric, who was greeting friends streaming down from several rows up into the theater. Everyone was overflowing with emotion, and no one, it seemed, any longer felt the need to observe the boundaries between the audience and the table. It was still an odd sight, David thought, watching the king of Israel embrace Dr. Carver—the "Ethiopian."

David turned and was almost bowled over by his favorite twelve-year-old. Anne Frank had come down the aisle as fast as she could, and now, close at last to her friend, she leaped into David's arms, and he whirled her around.

Placing her feet back on the floor, David laughed as Anne began to speak. He had forgotten how she went from one topic to another, chattering without slowing down. "I am so proud of you," she said. "I am proud of you all. King David is my friend too. Can you believe that you both have the same name? Were you aware that I knew him? Mrs. Meir introduced us. Do *we* have time to talk? Do you get to stay?"

As Anne drew a breath to continue on, David saw her countenance falter. Her smile, which had been so intense just a moment before, wavered as a question formed in her eyes. It had been only a second since she glanced away, but she looked past him now with a confused expression.

Quickly, David turned to see what had caught Anne's attention. The celebration was still in full force except, he saw immediately, for a few who wore the same questioning look on their faces. The odd reaction amid all the hoopla made him search quickly for the object of their attention. "What is it?" David asked Anne. "What's wrong?"

With her eyes and head, she indicated a direction for David to look. When he did, the same expression formed on his face. Now, around the room, the celebrations subsided, and it became noticeably quieter as first one small group then another became aware that something was wrong.

President Lincoln had not risen from his chair. In fact, it looked as if he hadn't moved. He was certainly not smiling—not even close. His gaze was fixed firmly on Gabriel, who David now saw had not moved either.

Everything had all happened so quickly, and now David's mind was racing to remember just exactly what *had* happened. He had answered the question . . . the archangel confirmed the answer . . . the relief washed over everyone . . . the celebration began . . .

As total silence overtook the theater, David saw that Gabriel was no longer smiling and was returning the gaze of the president as if each knew what the other was thinking. *No longer smiling*, David thought. Then a cold wave of fear washed over him. *He smiled*, David suddenly realized. Barely able to breathe, David was still working it out in his mind. *Gabriel smiled. He only smiled. We assumed . . .*

The archangel broke the silence in the room, but not his eye contact with the sixteenth president of the United States. "Do you have a question?" he asked.

Without moving, the president said simply, "The answer was incorrect?"

"Yes, Abraham Lincoln," Gabriel responded, "the answer was incorrect."

Lincoln nodded slowly. There was certainly nothing else to say, and the air had gone out of the room in any case.

The archangel looked around the theater and said, "As always, you are welcome to continue your conversations in this place or in any of the other locations that are provided." Looking to David, he remarked, "Assuming that you might wish to stay a while longer, I will leave now. I will return soon to escort you home." With that, the archangel moved toward the door, which had begun to open.

David had been horrified before, but now he felt a rising fury. It was inconceivable to him that the archangel would play with them in that way—that he would deliberately allow them to believe all was saved when, in fact, all had been lost.

David opened his mouth to speak, but he stopped as Gabriel turned at the door.

As angry as he was at that minute, David still managed to catch something in the archangel's eyes that prevented him from speaking out. Instead, he heard the strangest confession he ever could have imagined.

"Travelers," Gabriel said, "as a divine being, I have never been required to experience sorrow or sadness. Joy, yes. Excitement, yes. A sense of duty, yes. What you refer to as your feelings of sadness or remorse are simply not in my nature. As I have told you before, I am a servant."

He looked at Joan. "When I attended you on earth so many years ago, I did so at His behest. Please know that it was *joy* with which I paid you heed. Even at the fire, your body was fearful and I knew not how to help, so I showed you my joy. Do you remember?" When Joan nodded, he said, "And I was indeed joyful, for I knew that your time of suffering was at an end.

"Moments ago, it was not my intention to mislead you with the joy I expressed. Turning to David, he said, "So many times with the Travelers, I have wished to know how you feel. You are so strange to me . . . My momentary thought was one of joy for your accomplishment."

"Gabriel," David said rather coldly, "we accomplished nothing."

The archangel looked perplexed. "I have tried so hard to understand human beings. I assumed you *believed* that there is value in struggle. You say—I myself have *heard* you say—that the winds of adversity fill the sails of accomplishment."

Someone groaned. David was angry again. He couldn't help it. "That is a saying, Gabriel. It's a quote. I don't know who said it—probably someone in this room—but it is just a saying."

"I don't understand," Gabriel said.

David wanted to scream. He had rarely been this frustrated with anyone in his life. *I cannot believe*, he said to himself, striving desperately to remain calm, *that I am standing here trying to explain 'encouragement' to an archangel.* "It's an adage, Gabriel. A platitude. It is just something you say to someone so that they will fight on even when everything looks hopeless!"

The archangel furrowed his brow, thought for a moment, and said, "Oh."

Then he turned and walked through the door.

If David had been angry before, it was nothing compared to this. If he had been able to lay his hands on something, he would have thrown it.

Winston's face was a deep red. "I'd like to punch that angel right in the wings," he said.

"I understand how you feel," Joan replied, "but trust me; don't ever try. And he's an—"

"I know, I know," Churchill mumbled and walked away.

"I suppose I feel . . . well, hurt," Carver said. "I have worked with Gabriel myself—several times—and I never expected to be mocked." He paused and thought for a moment, then said to Eric. "That's what he did; isn't that right? He turned our words on us and walked out. I *never*," he repeated, "*never* expected to be mocked."

"I'm used to *humans* acting crazy," Eric said, "but I'm with you. I never expected that from an archangel."

Around the theater, it was the same in every gathering. The Travelers were hurt, angry, and confused. They seemed to seek some kind of understanding or comfort by gathering in groups of their peers. Bear Bryant was standing with John Wooden and Jesse Owens. Coach Bryant laid a hand on David's shoulder and squeezed as he walked by.

David sat down heavily in one of the theater seats. Across the room, Lincoln and Churchill were standing with Adams, Jefferson, Golda Meir, and Churchill's old friend, FDR. George Washington and Teddy Roosevelt were surrounded by another cadre of presidents and world leaders.

David was by himself. The other Travelers, it seemed, were giving him a moment to gather himself. *Or they're avoiding me because I blew it*, David thought darkly. Near the table, Red Grange and Jim Thorpe talked quietly with Babe Didrikson Zaharias, while behind him on row four, Edison and Einstein were still at it. Anne sat down next to David and, taking his hand in hers, never said a word.

Together they watched as people drifted around the theater, greeting old friends and talking quietly. Bob Hope, Bing Crosby, and Lucille Ball. Napoleon Hill, Og Mandino, and Noah—or Moses (David couldn't tell the difference). It would have been fun if he had not felt so miserable.

Benjamin Franklin sat down on the other side of Anne. Removing his spectacles, he wiped them with a handkerchief and perched them back upon his nose. He smiled at David and sighed. "I don't know what to say." He motioned around the room and added, "I don't think they do either, but I want to tell you that all of us thought you performed admirably. It was a difficult task, Mr. Ponder. None could have done better."

David was about to say, "Thanks" or "What does it matter?" or any one of the ten other things that were running through his mind, when a wadded-up piece of paper sailed over their heads and landed in the middle of the floor. Anne, David, and Franklin turned to see where it had come from, and it was obvious at first glance that either Einstein or Edison had thrown it. The two scientists were almost nose to nose.

Anne stepped out into the floor to retrieve the trash. While she was out of earshot, David whispered irritably to Franklin, "What in the hell are they arguing about?" The statesman peered over the top of his eyeglasses. "First of all," Franklin said, "don't curse. And *especially* not with *that* word. Not here." He smiled. "Many of us made it in by the skin of our teeth—a decision at the last moment—and would rather not be reminded of how close we came to the alternate destination."

Anne returned and sat back down. It appeared to David that after she had picked up the trash—something his daughter would have done when she was twelve, he thought—that Anne had looked for a place to deposit it. *Not a trash can in the whole place, I'll bet,* David thought to himself and held out his hand to Anne. He couldn't help but smile when again, just like Jenny would have done, the little girl put the trash in his hand without another thought.

Shoving the paper ball into his pants pocket, David was distracted again by the two men behind them. "No kidding," he said to Franklin. "What are they bickering about?"

Franklin laughed and shifted in his chair. Without even looking behind him, he said, "Same old thing. This time with a different twist. I think that's why they are so worked up."

"What same old thing?" David asked.

The founding father sighed. "Thomas Edison was afraid of the dark. Many people never knew this about him. He was ashamed—"

"Wait," David interrupted. "The guy who invented the lightbulb was afraid of the dark?"

Franklin dipped his head and peered over his spectacles again. "Why do you think he worked so hard to succeed at that particular task?" He relaxed again. "In any case, yes, that is quite true. Thomas Edison was afraid of the dark. Some folks on earth knew, of course, but *here* it is common knowledge. In fact, Thomas is quite proud of it."

"Why would he be proud of that?" David asked.

"Because it became his greatest asset in the specific task of inventing the first lightbulb. And that task, when he finally succeeded, became his greatest accomplishment. I'm sure you've heard the story." Franklin leaned in. "Thomas still tells it ad nauseam, doesn't he, Anne?" The girl giggled and nodded. "Thousands of failures before 'Eureka!' and he invented the lightbulb." Franklin had thrown his hands into the air when he said, "Eureka" in an apparent imitation of Edison. Anne doubled over laughing.

Concluding, Franklin said, "So that is the basis of his argument to Albert. And that is what he is hammering away at today. He contends that fear and adversity should lead to action. And that man should continue to act against fear and adversity, creating breakthrough after breakthrough until he is dead. Edison eventually obtained 1,093 patents for his inventions, you know."

Franklin looked at Anne and did his Edison impression again. "And what if I had quit? What if I had given in to my doubts and fears? Where would the world be today?" This was the funniest thing Anne had ever seen. Actually, despite his mood, David thought it was pretty funny too.

David glanced at the scientists again. "So . . . what? Edison thinks we should still be working on the answer to the question Gabriel posed?"

Franklin shrugged. "And that brings us to Albert. No one else *but* Albert would dare argue *anything* with Thomas Edison, of course. But Albert says, 'The significant problems we face cannot be solved at the same level of thinking with which we created them.'"

"I believe that," David said. "If a person does not grow and change and become more . . . well, I believe that."

"As do I," Franklin said. "But Albert argues that, except for you, they have put the wrong people in charge of solving the problem."

David frowned. "Except for me? Wrong people? What does that mean?"

The statesman grinned. "Don't you see? Albert contends that *we* are the wrong people to solve this 'significant problem' because *our* 'level of thinking' should be fixed."

Again, David frowned and shook his head, so Franklin tried again to explain. "Albert says our level of thinking should be fixed . . . unalterable . . . settled . . . permanently without forward motion. Because we are *here*. His assertion is that when we arrived *here*, our ability to expand our level of thinking—in earthly terms—was finished. So Albert says that you could have been left at home and worked this out yourself."

"Hmm," David mused. "So who do you believe?"

Franklin glanced around to make sure he wasn't overheard. "Edison."

"Why Edison?" David asked.

"Because," Franklin explained, "I have learned never to doubt the wisdom of Gabriel. He is a servant, correct? I mean, how often does he say that? And to doubt the servant would be to doubt the One he serves. You were brought here for a reason, my friend." He paused, then added, "It is hard to go against Albert, though. He was obviously right about the time travel thing."

"So I was brought here for a reason," David said. "Was the reason to fail?"

"No, of course not," Franklin insisted. "Back to Gabriel. To doubt the servant would be to doubt the One he serves! Gabriel did not bring you here to fail, because you were not created for failure! David Ponder, remember who you are. You are Everyman! You were created to learn, to become . . . to fight the winds of resistance. You were created to succeed!"

"Then why did we—why did I fail?"

"I don't know," Franklin said, frowning and shaking his head. "There is something more. I just know it. Have you ever had that little tingle just outside the realm of your consciousness . . . a word you couldn't remember . . . something you just couldn't get a handle on?"

David nodded.

"That is how I have felt ever since the archangel walked out of the theater."

"I've just been mad," David said, and Franklin chuckled.

For a time, they simply sat there. Franklin crossed his arms and physically relaxed. He closed his eyes and seemed to have retreated from their conversation. Anne held David's hand, and the two watched as the Travelers moved across the room from one group to the next. *There is no urgency in their voices or their movements now*, David thought. *It is over.*

About five minutes had passed when, suddenly, Franklin opened his eyes, stood up, and reached to get David to his feet. The man who helped form a nation had taken David by the arm and said, "Quickly. Come with me."

David and Anne followed Franklin, who passed Lincoln and asked formally, "Mr. President, would you join us, please?"

Lincoln glanced at David, who shrugged and followed Franklin with David and Anne seeing Benjamin Franklin walking so briskly against the backdrop of unmoving people caught Churchill's attention. Winston was curious and also joined the small group.

Franklin stopped at the table beside the hourglass and asked dramatically, "What do you see?"

David spoke for the rest. "An hourglass?"

"Not just *an* hourglass, my fine friend." Franklin arched his brow mysteriously. "This," he said," is *the* hourglass."

They all looked again. "Right," Winston said. "It is *the* hourglass that has been sitting here the whole time we've been talking."

"No, no, no," Franklin said to him, shaking his head back and forth. "Don't be dense. Look at it."

They did. And again, they looked back to Franklin. Still nothing.

Franklin inhaled deeply and exhaled with a big whoosh. "All right, people . . . ," he said as if warning them not to get this wrong again. "In relation to the amount of sand with which you began this little party, how much sand is in the upper half of the hourglass at this time?"

They looked closely, and Winston said what David had been thinking. "There's a bit less."

"Exactly!" Franklin exulted. "I thought so. Not always having the hourglass within my own sight, it was hard for me to keep track of just how much sand was falling. And I *do* keep track of time, you know." They looked at him blankly. "'Do not squander time, for that is the stuff of which life is made'? 'Time is money'? 'Lost time is never found again'? 'You may delay, but time will not'?" He looked at them expectantly. Again, there was no recognition in their faces. "Oh, come now," he said. "Those are *my* quotes . . . *my* adages. Surely you must have heard some of—"

Franklin had not seen Winston wink at Lincoln. He cleared his throat, dropped the subject, and continued. "The point I was *trying* to make was that I have a particular interest in the passage of time. Always have. So I sat in the theater, worrying as you at the table laughed and joked and told stories to each other *about* each other. It was enough to make me come out of my skin!

"But every time I managed a good look at the hourglass, it seemed to me that you had plenty of time left."

Winston frowned. "It was shoved down my way, you know. Right in front and a bit to the left of me. I glanced at it often as well, and several times I thought my eyes were playing tricks on me. Like you, I thought, *We are wasting time here.*

But again, there always seemed to be enough sand. As if we were in no danger of it running out." He paused and thought. "Except for that one time."

"When?" Franklin asked. "*Exactly* when?"

Winston looked at the others as if he were trying to remember the specific moment. "It was after Gabriel had given us the lecture. As I recall, he had gone and we were talking about the black dog." He looked at David. "You were discouraged—we all were, actually—and we began to discuss depression."

The others nodded, and Churchill continued, still deep in thought. "Right at the first of that discussion, I looked at the hourglass and thought it almost empty. I turned back to you all and was looking for an opening to tell you all to forget the conversation, just get the next Traveler out here! A minute or two later, I looked back and the sand was higher in the top again.

"So I began to keep an eye on it." He shrugged one shoulder. "Frankly, I have always considered myself a bit daft—I know I can't see well—therefore, I never said anything."

"You are not daft, Winston," Franklin said. "Not in this place, you aren't. As I said before, I now believe this to be *the* hourglass. Humanity's hourglass."

David frowned in disbelief, and Franklin said, "Why not? Why would He not put humanity's hourglass right in front of us? From the beginning, we have been assured that humanity possessed the power of choice."

"Think with me," Franklin said. "When humanity behaves wisely, is it conceivable that there might be more time in humanity's hourglass? When humanity behaves foolishly and with contempt, might humanity be on a shorter rope?"

Franklin looked from one to the other as they stood in the middle of the theater. He could tell they were buying into what he was suggesting. He pointed to the hourglass and said, "Look at it! This is the timepiece of mankind!"

Then his face went white. "Oh no," he said to himself. "Oh . . . no." The group huddled closer to Franklin in an effort to hear what he was saying.

"What?" Lincoln asked. "What's wrong?"

"Look at the sand," Franklin said intently. "Look at the sand."

What he had seen—what they now saw—was that the sand in the top half of the hourglass, while still there, had dropped precipitously.

"We see, Franklin," Lincoln said with urgency and concern in his voice. But they did *not* see. They had to be told.

"Two things very quickly now," Franklin said with a tremble in his voice. "One: time is running out. See?" He pointed and they nodded. "Two"—Franklin looked at them—"there is still time.

"Gentlemen . . . and ladies," he said, addressing Joan and Anne, "there is still time. If sand still remains in the hourglass of mankind, then there is still time for mankind."

"But we used up all five chances to answer," David said.

Lincoln jumped in. "I don't think that matters, David," he said. "All that with Gabriel . . . what did he say?" The president's mind was working desperately. He cocked his head as if he had pulled from his memory exactly what he intended to find. Then he smiled. "Gabriel said, 'I thought you *believed* there was value in the struggle.' Then he said something about 'the winds of adversity filling the sails of accomplishment.'

"We were put off by his statements, for we thought he was throwing our own words in our faces." Lincoln narrowed his eyes and looked closely at David. "But when you said, 'Those words are something you say to someone so that they will fight on even when everything looks hopeless,' that was enough for the archangel, and he left. Gabriel was telling us to fight on, even though everything looked hopeless."

Lincoln turned his eyes to Franklin and pointed to the hourglass. "You are right, my friend," he said. "There is still time."

CHAPTER 12

"Call them together and tell them what's going on," David said to Franklin. "They'll listen to you."

"Ladies and gentlemen!" Franklin said without delay. "Ladies and gentlemen, please take your seats. There has been a development."

Quickly, people moved to their seats. "Ladies and gentlemen," Franklin said over the noise, "please take *any* seat. Just sit down, please. Time is of the essence!"

At the table, where the chairs were filled with the original occupants, Winston was already grousing to David and Lincoln. "Well, why couldn't he have just come out and said it? Why not say, 'Fellows, we have a little extra time on the clock. Be my guest. Take another shot at it'? Why all the drama?"

"Ladies and gentlemen." Franklin was speaking again from the end of the table—the position most had come to think of as Gabriel's place. "Without taking the time to go into the wherefores and why-arts," he said, "let me get right to the point: we have more time to complete this task."

He pointed to the hourglass. "As you can see, there is still sand in the upper half, though we have now determined its fall rate to be somewhat increased since the archangel left the room. Don't make me explain it. Let's just get to it."

Franklin peered over his eyeglasses, examining the room. "Anne? Where did Anne go?"

"Here, sir," came the voice from the young girl. She had her hand raised from the second row.

"Help me, Anne," Franklin said. "Please, come here." As she approached the table, Franklin said to the crowd, "We've been all over the room with each other by now, so we might as well forget *that* rule."

He turned to Anne. "Dear? Please, if you don't mind, settle yourself right here beside me." He reached out and moved the hourglass to a position directly in front of her. "You are the proper height," he said, "to monitor the level of sand. Interrupt as you please, dear child, but keep us informed as to the time we have left."

Addressing the large audience again, Franklin said, "I believe another rule with which we can dispense is the edict against mingled conversation. With Mr. Ponder's consent, I move we allow anyone to speak during the time we have left." David signaled his agreement.

"Please . . . please!" Franklin said loudly as everyone began to talk at once. "We must do this in an orderly fashion. Let's hurry, but *please*, one at a time!" He pointed. "President Truman."

Truman stood from the third row behind David. "Responsibility should be considered. I'll sit down and let you take it from here."

"Excellent," Franklin said. Withdrawing writing utensils from his coat, he turned to David. "Mr. Ponder," he said, "exchange places with me, if you will. I propose to record the suggestions so that we have a basis for discussion. You, sir, are the leader of this summit. Take this position, sir."

David moved to the place that Gabriel, then Franklin, had occupied. It occurred to him to sit back down and allow someone else—anyone else—to lead the gathering. He was beyond discouraged or angry or confused. David was numb. But during his life, there was one thing the Seven Decisions had proven to him over and over again . . . He knew that victory did not always go to the smartest or the best looking. Breakthrough—physically, financially, emotionally, spiritually, and in every other way—came to the person who persisted without exception.

So even though he wanted desperately to quit, to let someone else lead, to slide into the background, David squared his shoulders, took a deep breath, and started over. "Okay!" he said, forcing a chuckle he did not feel. "We know what the answer is *not*, and we have a better understanding of the time issue, so I'd say we are in a much better spot than we were a few minutes ago." Several laughed, and there was a smattering of applause.

"Anne," he said, indicating the hourglass to the young girl, "where are we?"

"I don't know the time *exactly*, of course," she answered, "but the sand is falling at a steady pace."

David thanked her, then held up his arms and swept the crowd with his hands. "Ideas? Anyone? Let's go!"

As Travelers across the theater began to rise and speak, David glanced down at Lincoln, who gave him a nod and a proud smile. Winston waggled his eyebrows and flashed him a V sign with his fingers. It was Churchill's trademark: the V-for-victory symbol of his fight against the Nazis. With it, he had inspired the world.

"Forgiveness," Mother Teresa said, and there were several cries of, "Second!" in her wake.

"Let's discuss fairness," said Eleanor Roosevelt. She also had her supporters.

All across the theater, as fast as Franklin could write, one after the other, answers were proposed. "Never quit!" Martin Luther King said.

"Second! That's it!" followed his words from several voices.

"Kindness!" someone said behind David.

"Tolerance!" someone called, which was followed almost immediately by "A sense of humor!"

"Charity or prudence!" called another. "Write them both down!"

They never stopped to discuss anything in great detail, and as the ideas began to slow, so did the enthusiasm they had felt at still being in the game. Somehow, all the Travelers seemed to know that their answers were only different versions of those that had already been considered—that had already been rejected.

Several times, David had looked to Anne for guidance on the amount of time they might still possess, but the tiny girl only caught his eye once, and that was to give him a confused shrug. The other glances he took only revealed her scowling concentration.

After a pause in which the theater had grown silent, Franklin looked up from his task. To David, he said, "Is that it? Should we discuss these now?"

David answered by asking the assembly, "Does anyone have anything else they would like to submit? I believe we need to—" He stopped. Without warning, Anne had reached up and grabbed his arm fiercely. Looking down, he could see that she had not removed her gaze from the hourglass and, in fact, was still looking at it.

Anne got her face a little closer to the object and pulled David down with her. Lincoln and Churchill being the closest, they also stood and leaned over the table to see what the twelve-year-old had spotted. "Look," she whispered as she pointed to the top half of the glass.

What had startled her was obvious, and now an icy chill filled David's very being. The sand from the top had begun to flow rapidly through the constriction into the bottom of the device. For a reason they didn't dare stop and determine, the sand, which had been flowing at a steady rate since they had begun close observation, had now begun to surge through the aperture as if someone had enlarged the opening. "It will be over in five minutes at that rate," Winston said.

David turned to the audience, most of whom were now standing to see what was happening. "The sand," he said with a growing panic, "has apparently—well, it has *definitely*—

increased its rate of fall. I don't know why, but we need to figure this out quickly. Anyone?"

Joan left her chair and went to join Anne. She put an arm around the girl as they both monitored the hourglass. Eric, Carver, and King David hovered nearby.

"Anyone?" David pleaded again. "Does anyone have anything?"

"Should we call Gabriel?" someone said. "If we asked—"

Anne and Joan interrupted, speaking over each other in alarm. "It's speeding up! The sand is falling faster!" they said.

"No," David muttered. "Oh no." But it was true. If the sand had been falling fast before, now it was blistering a pace from the top of the glass to its bottom.

Around the hourglass, all those from the table were gathered closely. Several from the theater seats had also come close. They were frozen. They were out of time. "Sixty to ninety seconds, I would estimate," Franklin said.

"Sixty for certain," Winston whispered. "Look. It is actually speeding up."

Some in the theater turned around as if they couldn't bear to see—it seemed so strange to even say it—the end of time.

"Thirty, I would imagine," Lincoln said softly.

Tears flooded David's eyes as the top of the glass began its final whirlpool to emptiness. *Ten*, David thought. He was caught somewhere between anger and despair. He didn't know whether to curse or cry. *Five . . .*

"Do something!" a voice cried. "Do something!" It had

come from the darkness of the theater, somewhere in the rows beyond five or six. David wheeled on the sound and actually took several steps toward the area of the offender. His fury boiled over in that instant. *After all this time*, he thought. *All this work and someone has the gall to tell us to—*"

"David!" Lincoln barked. David knew he had crossed the line. He had shown his lack of self-control to everyone, and now the president was calling him down.

But that wasn't it at all. As David turned back, knowing now that it was all over, he met the incredulous stares of his friends. "David," Lincoln said in an astonished voice, "it stopped."

David frowned. "What stopped?" he asked.

"The sand," Lincoln said, pointing to the hourglass. "It stopped."

Slowly, as if afraid to move, David returned to the table. Benjamin Franklin had his face close to the glass, examining it very carefully. He put a finger up as if to tap it, and Winston slapped it away. "Don't do that," he said. "Don't bloody breathe on it!"

It was true. For some reason David could not determine, the sand had stopped flowing. There was definitely sand in the top of the glass, but it was motionless. Even the tiny, dry whirlpool was still intact.

Eric spoke. "I really don't even want to bring up this possibility," he said, "but is something stuck in it?"

No one knew.

"Exactly when," Franklin asked Anne and Joan, "did the sand stop?"

The girls agreed. "The sand stopped immediately," Anne said, "right after the man yelled."

Many more people had made their way to the floor now. The whole theater, it seemed to David was crowding around the table to get a glimpse of the hourglass that had ceased to flow with only seconds remaining.

"What did he yell?" David asked. "'Do something'? Didn't he yell, 'Do something'?" Heads were nodding all around, but no one had any idea why someone crying out in desperation at a critical moment would have gained a reprieve, if indeed that was actually happening.

David felt more than heard the movement behind him and turned as a man said his name. "Mr. Ponder?" the man said.

The man looked familiar, but David couldn't figure out why or how. He was an older gentleman with gray, almost white hair. He had a long, drooping mustache that, while it would be out of place on another person, looked elegant on him. He wore a gray suit that showed off the color of his hair, and around his neck he wore a string tie, a black one.

As they all stared, the man said, "Do something."

This was obviously the same man who had yelled from the audience and had now made his way to the table. David felt that same surge of anger that he had experienced moments before. Whether this man seemed familiar to him or not, this was not the time to interrupt, David thought, and was about to say so, when the man spoke again.

"We met at Gettysburg, Mr. Ponder," the man said. "I am Joshua Chamberlain. And the answer, sir, is 'Do something.'"

For a moment, everyone continued to stare at the new arrival. Most did not recognize his name, but David did. The anger left him immediately, and he reached out to shake Chamberlain's hand. "Joshua," he said. "It's good to see you. I'm sorry I didn't recognize you. We are both a bit older than the last time we met." Chamberlain chuckled politely.

"Joshua," David said and gestured to the group gathered around. "Please explain what you said. I'm afraid we don't understand. Is this . . . whatever you said . . . really the answer?"

Chamberlain pointed to the hourglass. "I believe so," he answered, inhaled deeply, and began. "It came to me at the last second. I was up on the eighth row—in the dark—and every time you took a break, something nagged at me. It wasn't until just a moment ago that I realized exactly what that was.

"As time was running out *here*, I remembered another moment in my life when time was running out. It was at Little Round Top, Gettysburg—July 2nd, 1863—when the enemy was coming up the hill for what would surely be the last time. My men—three hundred that morning, at this point shot down to eighty—were out of ammunition.

"My first thought was to hunker down behind the wall and wait. I must confess that with all the heroism talk about me that has gone on since that day—at *that* moment, I did not know what to do. So, in effect, I was about to give an order . . . to do nothing.

"At that very instant, a voice roared in my head. Until I arrived here, I always considered the voice to have been a result of battle trauma or an overactive imagination. But the voice yelled the words twice." Chamberlain paused abruptly, thinking hard, and added, "Yes, the voice yelled the words twice . . . just like I did a few minutes ago.

"The voice—now I know it was Gabriel—shouted the tiny phrase with an accent first on one word, then the other. '*Do* something,' he said. Then, 'Do *something*!' So I did. I pulled my sword, stood up on the wall, and ordered my men to charge.

"The rest, of course, you know. You were there." He shrugged. "The enemy threw down their weapons and ran. We had eighty men, and in three minutes we had captured four hundred of them."

Chamberlain shook his head in amazement. "*Now* I've heard all the stories about what happened because of that particular charge. Historians say that without our charge, the South would have won at Gettysburg. If the South had won there, they would have won the war, and it would've been over by the end of the summer.

"Historians say that had the South won, there would've eventually been several countries spread across the North American continent. And had that been the case, when Hitler swept across Europe in the 1940s, there would not have been a United States of America to stand in the breach. When

Hirohito invaded the islands of the Pacific, there wouldn't have been a *united* anything, much less a country big enough and strong enough to fight two wars on two fronts at the same time for the protection of the rest of the world."

Chamberlain lifted his eyebrows and smiled humbly. "And don't pat me on the back for any of it. I'm just as amazed as anyone. In a nutshell, all that I just described happened because, when I did not know what to do, I did *something.*"

Franklin spoke up. Still keeping an eye on the hourglass, he said, "Well, the sand stopped when he said those words." Everyone looked at each other as if to gauge reaction. Franklin said, "David?"

Looking to Lincoln, David asked, "Should we talk this out now or call Gabriel and talk it out in front of him?"

Lincoln looked at the hourglass, thinking, and finally said. "Let's call the archangel."

Before doing so, David informed the others and added, "Just stay where you are, or if you'd like to join us on the floor, please feel free to do so." He smiled. "We might as well break all the rules! By the way," he added, "if you have anything at all to say on this subject when he gets in here, do so. Let's leave nothing unsaid."

With agreement, determination, and anticipation on every face he could see, David said loudly, "I am ready with the answer!"

Without delay, the door swung open and Gabriel walked in. He had a deep frown on his face. "What is this?" he asked, stopping in front of David.

"We are ready with the answer, Gabriel," David said again.

"You have already used your five opportunities, David Ponder."

David lifted his chin. "Gabriel," he said, "with great respect, I ask you to please consider carefully what I am about to say. This will only take a moment." Without waiting for the archangel to acknowledge his request or to say whether he would or would not listen, David forged ahead.

"Sir," David said, "you told us at the beginning that we must fight with the weapons of wisdom and persuasion. I am not sure how much wisdom I have, but right now," he said with a smile, "I am mustering as much persuasion as I can."

David waited for Gabriel to smile in return. He did not.

"Gabriel," David said, "you told us that you alone were the arbiter of this summit. As the arbiter, you can decide whether or not we are able to present you with this answer. At one point earlier, I asked you if there was anything we could do to turn humanity back. Sir, you answered, 'Until it is too late, it is never too late.'" David pointed to the hourglass. "Gabriel," he pleaded with conviction, "*it is not too late.*"

With the barest hint of a smile, the archangel responded, "I will hear your arguments, followed by your final answer. I will reserve judgment on the admissibility of any of it until you are finished. At that point, it *will* be too late."

"Great," David said, trying not to show the relief he felt. "Thank you." Turning to Chamberlain, he prompted, "Joshua, why don't you get us started."

Stepping forward a bit, Chamberlain began. "Gabriel, I believe that when one doesn't know *what* to do, he should do *something*. At that moment of panic or discouragement, one cannot do *everything*, but he can do something. Will *doing something* change the world? I believe that this is what you meant when you said, 'It is the only thing that ever has.'" Chamberlain stepped back.

Lincoln raised his hand and spoke. "After the war, our nation's economy was in a shambles. It seemed that a full quarter of the population was out of work. No one, Gabriel, knew what to do. Most, of course, complained about the situation, about the war, and about me. In effect, I saw that they were complaining about the present, the past, and a person they did not know, who presumably held their job prospects in his hands.

"One afternoon, I was walking around Washington . . . " Lincoln turned to one of the more recent U.S. presidents who was standing nearby and added, "Some of us used to do that, you know." There were several chuckles from the audience. Seeing no response from Gabriel, Lincoln continued. "So there I was, walking with Mary, and a group of men approached us.

"These men were, they said, desperate for work. No jobs, they said. They told me they had tried everything. I asked what they did when they weren't looking for work. One man told me he stayed at home when he wasn't looking for work. Several men said they built a fire on a vacant lot and sat beside it. Two of them confessed they were so depressed that they had stopped seeking jobs at all."

Lincoln frowned for a moment, then opening his eyes widely, he said, "I didn't know what to tell them. I didn't know what to do, but this is what I said: 'Men,' I told them, 'you simply cannot sit around wasting your *unused* time. Continue to look for work, but in the time you have left, do something. *Anything*.'

"I said to them, 'The challenge I see in your eyes is that you have forgotten the value you possess as a human being. You have forgotten the value with which the Almighty created you. So what value do you have?' I pointed to one of them. 'You there,' I said. 'Can you read?' and he indicated that he could. 'Then find someone who can't, and read to them. Read to the blind, the elderly, the illiterate. Do something!'

"To another I said, 'You look very strong. Can you carry things?' 'Yes,' he replied. 'Then find people who need things carried, and do it! Men, listen carefully,' I said. 'I am not suggesting you find someone who needs weeds pulled and ask if you can pull them for a dollar. No! I am saying go out into your communities, find weeds that need pulling . . . and pull them!

"'I believe that you men will see amazing things happen in your lives. As you *do* something, you will renew your belief in yourselves. You will remember again the value that you really have as human beings. And another, perhaps more important thing will occur. *Others* will begin to see value in you. No longer will you be the desperate person, the sad person, the out-of-work person.

"'As people watch you—and they always do—they will begin to say, "Have you noticed that fellow who is always reading for people? Have you seen the man who is always carrying things for others? Have you spotted the boy who is always fixing things for folks, who is always helping?" Men, I say to you now that as others watch, they will begin to place a value on you they never had before.'

"I winked at them and said, 'And you know what happens to people of value, don't you? They gain opportunities; they get help; they receive job offers. Why? *Because they did something when they didn't know what to do.*'"

Lincoln ended with, "I kept track of those men, and all did well with the concept. Three of them, curiously, managed to find a way to work for free for the companies with whom they had wanted to be employed. They figured that if they made themselves valuable, as a job came open, the company wouldn't look outside to hire. They figured—correctly, it turned out—that the company would hire *them*, for they had proven their value. By doing *something*."

Before Gabriel could take a breath, Franklin spoke up. "From our vantage point, we have watched humanity with concern for some time now. Mankind has become divided. That is obvious. Mankind is now divided culturally, racially, religiously, financially, and politically.

"There was a time, in the not-so-distant past, when humanity's leaders would argue points and philosophies, then retire to dinner together, laughing and inquiring as to the well-being of the other's family. This no longer happens.

"It appears to me," Franklin said as he glanced around

to the others, "that people have retreated from their front porches only to build enclaves encircling singular points of view. So what might be the remedy to this particular challenge? I believe the remedy might just be what President Lincoln proposed to those men.

"Somehow, when we work side by side, differences don't appear so distinct. The wealthy and the downtrodden become acquainted. Each gains new respect for the other's position. Help and ideas begin to flow both ways."

Winston jumped in. "'Red and yellow, black and white'— as the old song goes—'they are precious in His sight.' If that is true, and of course you and I know *now* that it is, then humanity ought to bloody well act like it!

"Conservative Party and Labor, Republican and Democrat . . . Franklin is right. They have become divided. It is no longer about the country. It is about themselves. And the only cure is for humanity to care again. To come out of their homes and away from their fenced-in lives. It is time to *do something*."

"There will be those," Teddy Roosevelt said loudly, "who will always moan and complain about where they are. I say, 'Do what you can, with what you have, where you are!' Humanity must remember: *almost everything* comes from *almost nothing*! Do something, I say, and do it now."

"'Do it now' is right!" shouted a female voice. It was Wilma Rudolph, the Olympic track star who had overcome childhood polio, measles, whooping cough, and scarlet fever to become one of the greatest athletes of the twentieth century. "Success begins," she said, "the moment we understand that success in anything is about beginning! Do something now!"

Thomas Jefferson said, "The question for each person to settle is not what he *might* do if he had the money, the influence, or the education, but 'What will a person do with the things he *has?*' To be discouraged about what you don't have is to waste what you *do* have." Jefferson looked at John Adams and George Washington, who were standing beside him. "We believe," he said to Gabriel, "that this at last, sir, is the answer: 'Do something.'"

Finally, the theater grew silent again. Everyone watched the archangel for some kind of reaction, but there was none. David said, "The question is, 'What should humanity do, individually and collectively, in order to restore itself to the pathway toward successful civilization?' The answer at which we have arrived, sir, contains in whole, every other virtue that we previously discussed.

"What should humanity do? Something. The answer, Gabriel, is 'Do something.'"

Gabriel stared hard into David's eyes. Finally, he said, "Would it be possible for you to put this answer in the form of a declaration?"

"Yes," David replied evenly. "Certainly we can."

"Do it," the archangel said and once again walked out without another word.

When Gabriel was gone and the door shut, everyone closed ranks. "I have the writing materials," Franklin announced, holding aloft parchment and pen.

"Was that a yes or a no?" Eric asked. "A correct or an incorrect?"

"That was a 'do it,'" Winston replied, "so let's have at it. Or as we are now proclaiming, we shall do *something*!"

After working for over an hour, the group had a manageable draft. They read it aloud and worked it over again. At last, after three more drafts, they were satisfied with what they believed summed up the philosophy quite well. "This will be a document," Lincoln stated, "that humanity, individually and collectively, will be able to read again and again. This will be our true legacy on earth: collected wisdom gathered into a single thought: 'Do something.'"

Gabriel was called back into the theater, and upon his return, the archangel simply asked to hear what they had written. David read it for them all.

A PERSONAL DECLARATION

Knowing that all those who "arrive" have to begin where they are, I choose to begin now. At this moment, I will do something.

For too long, I have allowed fearful thoughts to dominate my life. Now I recognize fear as a misuse of the creative imagination that has been placed inside me. In the past, I have allowed fear to shove all hope aside. No more! Fear no longer has any power to stop me from doing what I know to be right and true. I am no longer afraid. I am courageous. Right now, I will do something.

The person who faces no hardships gains no strength. Though I do not look for hardship, I am grateful for its results, for I have grown mighty in soil mixed with troubles. My roots are now deep. My mind and heart have become powerful. A beautiful flower cannot be created without fertilizer. A dazzling gem cannot be polished without great friction. I have taken the fertilizer and the friction and am better because of it. Now it is time for me to do something.

I cannot do everything, but I can do something. And I can do something right now. Never again will I allow what I cannot do to interfere with what I can do. Circumstances are rulers of the weak. I am not weak. Neither discouragement nor despair will stop me from doing something and doing it now. I am strong-minded. I can make myself do something I would rather not do, in order to get a result that I do want. I will do something. And I will do it now.

My life, which was once a question mark, is now a statement. Stormy seas do not scare me, for I am the calm in the storm. My past is behind me and my future is bright because I now know the secret of the present. I will do something and I will do it now.

Right now, I will do something for my family. Right now, I will do something for my friends. Right now, I will do something for those who do not even know my name. For my family, my friends, and the strangers of the world are valuable in my Creator's sight. I will let them know that I recognize that fact by my actions. I now know that my smile, my words, and my attitude are actions. They are all under my control. I am prepared to run my race. I am ready to hit the mark. I will now do my part in restoring humanity to the pathway toward successful civilization.

I will do something. And I will do it right now.

When David finished, he took the parchment and folded it once, then again. Offering it to the archangel, he said, "The answer, Gabriel, is 'Do something.'"

Gabriel held up his hands, palms toward David. Refusing the parchment, he said, "Do not give it to me, David Ponder. This is for humanity. Your answer is correct."

EPILOGUE

"You are home, David Ponder," Gabriel said.

David opened his eyes and saw that, indeed, he was back at his desk in Dallas, in the penthouse office. Reaching for a pitcher that was always there, he offered some water to Gabriel, who refused, and then poured himself a full glass. While he drank deeply and attempted to overcome the dizziness caused by his return, David's mind raced. *When did we leave? How long have I been gone? Did this really happen?*

Of course, with an archangel in front of him, that was an easy question to answer.

"I took you during the celebration," Gabriel said, as if reading his mind. "You did extraordinarily well, David Ponder."

"Thank you, Gabriel," David responded. "You were, at times, a tough guide."

"How would you say it?" the archangel asked with a smile. "'The winds of adversity fill the sails of accomplishment?' That is a saying, David Ponder. An adage. A platitude. It is simply something one says to people so they will fight on even when things look hopeless." David laughed and for the first time saw Gabriel do the same.

"Whew," David said. "I am still dizzy." Reaching into

his pocket for a handkerchief, he removed instead a ball of paper. Tossing it into the wastebasket, David found his handkerchief in the other pocket.

Gabriel furrowed his brow. "What was that, David Ponder?" he asked. "What just went into the trash?"

David was so tired that he had to think for a minute to remember what the archangel was asking about. He looked into the trash can. "Oh," he said. "I don't know. Just trash that fell on the floor in the theater. Anne picked it up. No trash can there, so I put it in my pocket."

"What is it?" the archangel asked again.

"Well, Gabriel," David said, attempting to keep the impatience from his voice, "I told you that I don't know." He reached down into the wastebasket. Retrieving the wad of paper, he quickly unfolded it and looked. "Just numbers," he said and handed it to Gabriel. "It looks like a math professor's bad dream."

The archangel took one look and shook his head irritably. He continued to read the page and shook his head again in quick little jerks. When he rolled his eyes, David said, "Okay. It's my turn. What is it?"

"This stays with me," Gabriel said and folded it into his robe.

"What's the deal here?" David said in a smart voice. "You had to ask me twice, so I have to ask you twice? What is it?"

The archangel pulled the page back out of his robe and opened it up. Flopping it at David as if it were a wilted stick, he said, "That Albert. Almost everyone obeys the rules, except Albert. I have to talk with him at least once a week. This is Albert's."

David held up three fingers. "Three times, friend," he said. "What is it?"

"Time travel," Gabriel said simply. "*We've* always been able to do it, of course, but Albert got so close to the formula while on earth that he hasn't been able to leave it alone."

"Is that it?" David asked with a grin. "Did he get it right?"

Gabriel nodded and narrowed his eyes. "But I'll never tell him so," he said with a smile. David laughed again.

"Good-bye, David Ponder. I will see you again," Gabriel said.

David stood. "Good-bye, Gabriel. Thank you . . . for everything."

"Do you have the declaration?" Gabriel asked and watched as David patted his jacket pocket and nodded. With that assurance, the archangel slowly extended his wings, arching them up for the mighty thrust that would take him away.

David stepped back. It was at that moment that Gabriel paused. Looking at the tobacco pouch and the other items on David's desk, he relaxed a bit, though his wings were still above his head. "Why do you keep those things, David Ponder?" he asked. "Do you not know the Seven Decisions by now?"

"Yes. I do," David said. "But I keep them all in the pouch, and every now and then, I take them out to touch, to feel." He gestured at the items with his hand. "They encourage me when I am down. They remind me to always depend on the truth." David smiled. "And they prove to me every day that this really did happen."

The archangel returned the smile. Then, after a moment's hesitation, he plucked a beautiful white feather from under his wing. The deep gold of the tip shimmered as he held it up to be seen. "Yes, David Ponder," Gabriel said as he placed the feather on the tobacco pouch, "*this really did happen.*"

And with a thrust of his wings and a burst of light, he was gone.

AUTHOR'S NOTE

I n hopes of adding to your experience and satisfaction with this book, I wanted to offer a bit more information. The following should answer at least two of the questions that might have been rolling around the edges of your imagination as David Ponder's story unfolded.

First, it is true that I am responsible for most of the words spoken by the historical characters. A very few of those words, however, are direct quotes from that character that I merely placed in context of the discussion. For instance, Winston Churchill really did refer to his depression as "the black dog," and while most of his conversation about the subject was created for the reader, the paragraph about him not standing near the edge of a platform at a train station and avoiding the rail of a ship was all his. Winston Churchill spoke precisely those words.

While conversations between the summit's participants were obviously created, the background information about each character is, without exception, absolutely true. And yes, that includes the facts about the life of Eric Erickson.

I wonder if you were as shocked reading about Erickson as I was uncovering the story of this unbelievable man! Every moment described in this book really happened, and again, just as I did while writing *The Heart Mender*, I constantly asked myself, "Why is this not in history books? How is it possible that no one seems to have heard this story?!"

The tale of Eric and his wife Ingrid was, without a doubt, the most frustrating research I have ever done on a subject for whom almost no information exists in a single location. Eric is mentioned here and there in old transcripts and in the records of both the Allies and Nazi Germany. And again, for the record, President Eisenhower and Albert Speer *really did* say that Eric Erickson was responsible for the ending of the war.

The one hugely interesting fact that for some reason I chose not to include in this book was actually the closest Eric ever came to being caught. By happenstance one evening while in Germany, Eric ran into an old acquaintance he had thought long dead. The man was suspicious of Eric's presence in Germany at that time and questioned him thoroughly. Midway through the conversation, the man suddenly began acting friendly and as if he believed everything he was hearing.

Not trusting the sudden change of heart he had observed, as they parted, Eric doubled back and followed his interrogator. Sure enough, the man stopped at the first pay phone he saw and began reporting to the Gestapo a traitor in their midst. Before the man could utter his name, Eric dragged him from the phone booth and into an alley. There, Eric killed the only person who ever suspected his true intentions . . . with a pocketknife.

Andy Andrews
Orange Beach, Alabama

ACKNOWLEDGMENTS

I am blessed to be surrounded by friends and family who have become a team of which I am thrilled to be a part. If I can ever be perceived as a person who makes good and informed choices, it is only because of my reliance on the wise counsel of these people. Thank you all for your presence in my life.

To Polly, my wife and best friend: Thanks for your love, wit, patience, and happy spirit.

To Austin and Adam, our boys: You guys are the best. I am so proud of who you are becoming. Remember to smile while you talk!

To Robert D. Smith, my personal manager and champion: After thirty years together, you still amaze me every day. And it's not just me—everyone thinks you are the best!

To Todd Rainsberger: your "story" advice is always appreciated. And fun!

To Scott Jeffrey: you are the Bear Bryant of "life coaches."

To Duane Ward and the whole incredible gang at Premiere Speakers Bureau: you are not just partners; you are friends.

To Gail and Mike Hyatt, who gave life to my career as an author: I am honored to call you friends.

To Jennifer Stair, my editor, whose careful eye and quick

mind made this a much better book: I very much appreciate your calm tact and great humor. To the dozens of people at Thomas Nelson who touched this book through marketing and sales.

To Matt Baugher, my publisher from Thomas Nelson: Thanks for your wise guidance and encouragement. In addition to being the best at what you do, you have become a great friend and definitely made "this author thing" a lot more fun.

To Kurt V. Beasley and Brent C. Gray, who handle the legal rights to all my intellectual property.

To Sandi Dorff, Paula Tebbe, and Susie White, who direct the daily parts of my life: without the effort, prayer, and attention to detail of you three ladies, my own efforts would not come to nearly so much.

To Nicholas Francis, Denny Swindle, and Zachary Smith: thank you for your Web mastery and simply making the Internet work. To Jared McDaniel and Kevin Burr: thanks for your sense of humor and unbelievable artistic ability—both in print and on the Web.

To Nate Bailey: many thanks for your organizational skills, happy demeanor, and "never say die" attitude. To Paul "Saul" Fries, Matt Lempert, Ben Mills, David Loy, and Will Hoekenga for their amazing behind-the-scenes work in the Nashville office. To Melinda and Christian Leake and Peggy Hoekenga for developing fantastic curriculum for this book and all the others.

To Mary Graham and all my buddies on the Women of

Faith tour: thanks for your laughter and encouragement!

To authors Gloria Gaither, Jack Higgens, Andy Stanley, and others too numerous to mention: your influence on my style is probably apparent, but I wanted to say thanks anyway.

To Paul Krupin and George and Margaret Uribe for their masterful ability to get the word out to the masses. To Greg and Sara Travis for their unrivaled capability to communicate stories through video.

Special thanks to Shannon and John D. Smith for the use of their little yellow cottage. It was the perfect place to write!

Thanks to Tammy and Bo Cross for the use of their awesome beach house during the two weeks the Smith cottage was unavailable!

To Katrina and Jerry Anderson; Vicki and Brian Bakken; Erik Born; Don Brindley; Sunny Brownlee; Foncie and Joe Bullard; Brent and Pam Burns; Bailey Callaway; Myrth and Cliff Callaway; Kayla Carter; Jennifer R. Casebier; Julie and Doug Cassens; Gloria and Bill Gaither; Lillian and Edward Gilley; Gloria and Martin Gonzalez; Greta and Greg Good; Bill Gothard; Lynn and Mike Jakubik; Kent Kirby; Deb and Gilbert Little; Nancy Lopez; Mark Lowry; Melanie and Mike Martin; Karen and Alan McBride; Liz and Bob McEwen; Edna McLoyd; Mary and Jim Pace; Glenda and Kevin Perkins; Brenda and Todd Rainsberger; Sharon and Dave Ramsey; Becky and Ted Romano; Barbara Selvey; Claudia and Pat Simpson; Shannon and John D. Smith; Jean and Sandy Stimpson; Dr. Christopher Surek; Marla and Dan Toigo;

READERS' GUIDE

Chapter 1

1. Make a list of the Seven Decisions. Which of these Seven Decisions is the hardest to apply to your life? Which of these Decisions is the easiest to implement? Explain your answer.

2. Looking back on your life, name one incident that you might regret. Of the Seven Decisions mentioned above, which one could have helped you the most in that situation? How can seeking wisdom help in these types of situations?

3. "Adversity is preparation for greatness." What does this mean to you, and how can it apply to your life?

Chapter 2

1. What would it be like to live "in truth" every day? Would this make your life harder or easier? Explain your answer.

2. In your own life, do you have memories for which you have "rewritten the history to make it more 'palatable'"? If so, why do

you think you have done so? Did it work for or against you in the long run?

3. Do you ever turn from the real truth to re-create your own version of truth? If so, does this ever help your future?

4. Has someone ever entrusted you with a seemingly overwhelming responsibility that you didn't think you were capable of handling? Did you try? If so, were you more capable than you had originally anticipated?

5. Why is David considered the perfect example of the human race or "common man"? List three reasons why David was chosen as a leader.

6. Do you ever use your personal "failures" to advance your own "wisdom's cause"?

Chapter 3

1. Up until now, have you experienced an "intermission" in your life? If so, reflect on that experience. What led up to this intermission? What steps did you take to move past the intermission and into the second act?

2. Reflecting on the question above, why is perspective such an important ingredient in moving forward to the second act?

3. Do you have a "memory of success" that might prompt and encourage you to a greater level of success in the future?

4. Have you experienced the "encouragement of success" and not come out of the Valley? What holds you back from moving forward? What obstacles are stopping you from succeeding?

Chapter 4

1. In order to start a second act, what would be your new direction? How can you begin that new course today?

2. How has your definition of success changed after reading this book? How does this new definition contribute to your success?

3. Is having success the same thing as having a successful life?

4. What did Churchill mean by the term "Principle of the Path"?

5. In the past, have you made decisions to have a life of success or a successful life? Which one is more important and why?

Chapter 5

1. Can you remember a time when you lived without hope? How did this affect your life? How did you restore your hope?

2. What does the word *hope* mean to you? Is hope more important to you after reading this book? Why or why not?

3. What did Joan say was the proof of hope? Do you agree?

Chapter 6

1. Prior to reading *The Final Summit,* what was your definition of wisdom? How has that definition changed?

2. How does wisdom differ from knowledge? Has there been a time in your life when you have mistaken wisdom for knowledge?

3. How have you gained wisdom? Has it been through imitation, as the Travelers suggested? Do you agree with David that imitation is "the easiest way to gain wisdom"?

4. How can you apply wisdom in your life? How will this help lead you to a life of success?

Chapter 7

1. How did Eric Erickson define courage? Do you think this definition can make it easier to be courageous?

2. Do you believe you have the "power" to achieve whatever you wish? How can a lack of courage get in your way?

3. Which has had more impact on your life, courage or cowardice? Explain your answer.

4. Do you agree with Joan that physical courage is more common than moral courage? Why is this (or is it not?) so? How do you define moral courage?

Chapter 8

1. What do you think Gabriel meant when he said humans are egotistical? Explain your answer.

2. According to Gabriel, why is the current civilization in peril? Do you agree that these reasons can destroy a civilization?

3. Do you ever rely on the idea of chance? Is relying on this idea a good thing or a bad thing? Why or why not?

4. What did Gabriel say chance has done to mankind?

Chapter 9

1. What did Churchill mean by the "black dog"? What does your "black dog" look like? Do you agree that it is always nearby?

2. According to Churchill, how can you get good answers? What did King David offer as the answer?

3. Why did King David practice self-discipline? How does self-discipline help remind you of what you really want in life?

4. What question did King David say "fuels a person" into self-discipline? Do you agree that self-discipline helps yield great rewards? Why or why not?

5. What is the best evidence for the power of self-discipline, according to King David? Are there things that you don't do because you lack self-discipline?

6. How would you answer the question, "What do you really want?"

7. Are self-sacrifice and self-discipline related? If so, how?

Chapter 10

1. What did George Washington Carver say would determine greatness?

2. Do you agree with Joan when she said, "Character is a thing we alone are responsible to form"? How do we form character? How would you describe your character?

3. What were Lincoln's definitions of *reputation* and *character*? How is character determined, and how is it built?

4. King David said, "Nothing shows a person's character more than his habits." What are your habits, and what kind of character do they portray?

Chapter 11

1. Why is the hourglass important? In what ways does behaving wisely versus foolishly have an effect on the "hourglass"? What was Gabriel's main point?

2. Do adversity and the feeling of hopelessness put "wind in your sails"? If not, what must you do to think this way?

3. Do you believe that you matter just as much as the next person in making more "time" for humanity? Why or why not?

Chapter 12

1. What caused the sand in the hourglass to stop?

2. Is it easier for you to be idle and waste your unused time when adversity strikes? Why?

3. Have you ever forgotten your value as a human being? What values do you believe human beings possess? Do you believe all humans have an equal value in this world?

4. Have you ever fenced in your own life? What could you do to show your value to others? What could you be doing "right now"?

5. Could you sign your name on the "personal declaration"?

6. What was the final answer?

The Final Summit experience doesn't have to end.

Inspired and ready to do something? Start here.

Unlock an exclusive video of Andy sharing never-before-heard insights behind the stories you've just read.

plus...

Teachers and book clubs: get your free companion curriculum.

www.TheFinalSummit.com/unlock

Contact Andy

To book Andy for corporate events, call

(800) 726-ANDY (2639)

For more information, go to

www.AndyAndrews.com
www.facebook.com/AndyAndrewsAuthor
www.twitter.com/AndyAndrews

ABOUT THE AUTHOR

ailed by a *New York Times* reporter as "someone who has quietly become one of the most influential people in America," ANDY ANDREWS is the author of *New York Times* best sellers *The Noticer* and *The Traveler's Gift*, and is also an in-demand speaker for the world's largest organizations. Zig Ziglar says, "Andy Andrews is the best speaker I have ever seen." *The Traveler's Gift* and *The Noticer* were featured selections of ABC's *Good Morning America*, have been translated into nearly twenty languages, and continue to appear on best-seller lists around the world. Andy has spoken at the request of four different United States presidents and toured military bases around the world, being called upon by the Department of Defense to speak about the principles contained in his books. Arguably, there is no single person on the planet better at weaving subtle yet life-changing lessons into riveting tales of adventure and intrigue—both on paper and onstage. He lives in Orange Beach, Alabama, with his wife, Polly, and their two sons.

For more information, visit www.AndyAndrews.com

The NOTICER

Sometimes, all a person needs
is a little perspective.

ISBN: 978-0-7852-2921-6

"The Noticer is completely absorbing. Anything less than stunning would be an understatement. This is not just one of the best books I have read . . . This is the best book I have ever read in my life."

N A N C Y   L O P E Z ,
L P G A   H A L L   O F   F A M E R

T H E
BUTTERFLY
E F F E C T

HOW   YOUR   LIFE   MATTERS

ISBN: 978-1-4041-8780-1

"Every single thing you do matters.
You have been created as one of a kind.
You have been created in order to make a difference.
You have within you the power to change the world."

A N D Y   A N D R E W S